# Taking Off Overcoats

# Taking Off Overcoats

## A Simple, Loving Approach to Awakening

Karen Anderson
and
Barry Martin Snyder

Luminous Self Media

Front cover artwork by Anna Oneglia
http://annaoneglia.com/

Luminous Self Media
http://www.luminousself.com

ISBN 978-0-9835990-6-7
Printed in the United States of America

# Contents

# Introduction

*seeker of truth*
*follow no path*
*all paths lead where*
*truth is here*

*e. e. cummings*

## The Time of Awakening is Now

It's a powerful time on planet Earth.

Millions of souls are in the process of awakening.

In the beginning, awakening souls may feel restless, or disillusioned, or inquisitive, or deeply confused.

Some have been thrust into the messy process of awakening when their worlds imploded.

Jobs lost, relationships over, money gone.

A huge heartbreak may have catapulted others into the throes of the meltdown that often begins the process of waking up.

Some feel compelled to leave their current life pattern in order to follow a dream that may seem wildly impractical, but cannot be denied.

Others have an inner hunch that more is possible, but are not sure what to do next.

Many seek a more meaningful life, a way of being based in eternal values, not current trends.

Whatever our outer circumstances, there comes a point in the journey through all our lifetimes when we somehow know there is *something more*.

The ways awakening unfolds vary, but the underlying dynamics are the same.

We begin to sense that there is more to life than the outer level of reality would indicate.

And that we are far more than the being we see in the mirror.

Often, the journey inward is catalyzed by suffering.

Wondering if there is a deeper meaning to our earthly dilemmas and struggles, we explore spiritual paths and practices.

We seek understanding, and hope to find wisdom.

Most of all, we want to experience more love and greater peace.

In short, we know that it is time to awaken out of the nightmare of suffering.

Even if we are not yet sure of what that even means.

## What Do We Mean by Awakening?

In this book, we discuss awakening in a simple, easy-to-grasp way.

For us, awakening consists of two mutually reinforcing processes:

1) Releasing our identification with who and what we are not,

which allows us to

2) Experience more of who and what we truly are.

Some describe this as the fundamental shift from seeing ourselves as the egoic, human self to realizing we are a divine, eternal soul.

The problem with this approach is that many of us have turned against the ego, believing it is bad and must be eradicated if we are to awaken.

This sets up an adversarial relationship that only gets in the way of awakening.

For this reason, we prefer to use different language for what is essentially the same process.

Rather than focusing on the ego, we will be talking about overcoats.

Since most humans have never heard awakening discussed in terms of overcoats, the chances are good that you carry few, if any, negative associations about that term.

This allows you to approach awakening from a neutral, open-minded standpoint.

That can only help the process to unfold with greater ease and grace.

## Is Awakening For You?

Many spiritual seekers believe that fully awakening in this lifetime is for the few, not the many.

Living in an awakened state may sound great, but seem impossible.

Compared to learning earthly skills, awakening may seem complicated and obscure.

Some seekers have tried to read spiritual books, only to find them hard to fathom or relate to.

Others believe awakening is difficult.

Their minds may be filled with beliefs like *It takes a long time* and *It requires a lot of effort.*

It may seem that awakening requires decades of arduous spiritual practice.

But you know what?

None of that is necessarily true.

This book was written for all who know that now is the time to awaken.

It is for those who are brave enough to imagine that awakening doesn't need to be complicated or take forever.

It was written for souls who know deep inside that if they want to awaken, they must be ready for that to happen.

We do not need to get a Ph.D in spiritual studies before it can begin to occur.

We are ready to awaken when we glimpse the possibility that we are meant to be happy, not to suffer our way through life.

In fact, that awareness means that awakening is already underway.

## How This Book will Best Support Your Awakening

This book was written to facilitate your awakening.

It presents a simple, effective way to use your "stuff" — whatever is going on within you and in your life — as a doorway to awakening.

If you are willing to show up with What Is — now, and now, and now -- this book will help you to use anything that is present as a springboard to awakening.

This is an experiential book.

It offers a step-by-step, sequential, integrated journey into awakening.

You will not only read about awakening — you will be an active participant in your own unique process of awakening.

It can be helpful to keep a notebook or journal nearby as you make your way through each chapter.

Writing about what happens within you as you travel through the book can expedite and enhance your awakening.

This is not a book to randomly dip into or skip around in.

It will most fully support your awakening when it is read and contemplated from start to finish.

Complete the entire journey, one chapter at a time.

Celebrate the awakenings that occur all along the way.

Then, if you like, you can return to specific chapters to delve more deeply into specific topics.

## To Get What is Here, Slow Down

Since there is a lot of white space around the words in this book, it might be tempting to read it quickly.

But rushing through the book is not advised.

It is meant to be slowly savored and absorbed over time.

Although most of the sentences are short and simple, a lot of evolutionary stimulation is packed into each one.

More opportunities for awakening are hidden between the lines, in the quiet spaces where shifts happen.

The purpose of *Taking Off Overcoats* is not to fill your mind with yet more information.

It has a far more significant purpose than that.

Reading this book is intended to activate your divine Self, and to spark your awareness of who you truly are.

*Taking Off Overcoats* contains a living transmission of the energy and consciousness of awakening.

Resist the temptation to speed-read the book, or that transmission may not have a chance to land within you.

Instead, approach *Taking Off Overcoats* with the unhurried spaciousness that is present in the book's layout.

Read this book in the same way you would take a quiet walk by a stream.

Imagine it's a long, Sunday afternoon with nothing else to do and no place else to be.

You have all the time in the world to savor everything you are feeling, seeing, and sensing within as you read.

Let the messages encoded within and between the words reveal themselves at their own pace.

As you travel through these pages, the inner process of awakening will be occurring.

Often, awakening may be happening beneath or beyond your conscious awareness.

From time to time, you may need to put the book down for a while, so that the next steps in your awakening can take place.

You will know when it is time to pick it up again and keep reading.

This is how you honor your own unique pace and process of waking up.

## Experiences of Awakening

*Taking Off Overcoats* contains a wealth of guided, inner Experiences designed to catalyze awakening.

As you come to each Experience, approach it slowly.

Not much will happen if you merely **read** the Experience.

Since many of the Experiences are short, it may be tempting to quickly read them and keep on going.

If you give the Experience just a few moments of your time, you will merely skim the surface of your awareness.

This is not likely to yield any very significant realizations about yourself.

Instead, allow plenty of time to drop into your inner world and be present with everything that is going on inside of you during each Experience.

When we drop below the thinking mind, we become aware of everything else that is happening within us.

We discover bodily sensations, emotions, memories, and "unfinished business" -- all of which want our attention.

This is the stuff of awakening.

We cannot gloss over it and expect to become more self-aware.

Give whatever arises all the time it wants and needs.

This is how we nurture our own process of awakening.

Engaging with the Experiences over time will help you to tell the difference between the voices of who you are not -- the voices of your overcoats — and the "still, small voice" of your soul.

Then you can choose which voice you want to listen to, instead of being run by the language of suffering.

As you read this book and work with the Experiences, you will come to know, through your own direct experience, that the Divine lives within you as your true Self.

You will experience yourself as a soul, a radiant being of light with a purpose for being here that no other soul can fulfill.

You can <u>download MP3 recordings of each Experience</u> on our website at https://www.luminousself.com/taking-off-overcoats-experiences.html

## Be Gentle with Yourself

The inner Experiences in *Taking Off Overcoats* are designed to help you integrate and embody the material in each chapter.

As you dive into these Experiences, beware of the mind's tendency to judge what happens.

Or what *doesn't* seem to be happening.

The mind may even conclude that you are "failing."

You may also come up against resistance.

A particular inner process may not seem easy or pleasant.

It may even take you into inner recesses of pain that a part of you would rather not face.

The mind may want to judge the Experience itself or make it wrong.

*This isn't working,* the mind might insist.

It may even loudly complain, *I don't like this!*

Do your best to observe these thoughts without giving them any power or reality.

Believing such ideas is optional, and not recommended.

Instead, keep in mind that the outer world is a noisy, chaotic place.

It is full of complex drama and blaring stimulation.

Since this is where most of us habitually focus our attention, when we turn our awareness inward we may conclude that not much is happening.

In contrast to the outer world of the senses, the inner realm of the soul is quiet and subtle.

Its depth and stillness may seem unfamiliar, and might feel strange or empty.

It may seem that something is missing.

Or, emotions that have waited a long time for your attention may roar to the surface.

The mind may try to convince you that this couldn't possibly be a good thing.

Yet coming to know what lives within us is an essential aspect of awakening.

Give yourself an all-important gift: drop any and all expectations and invite each Experience to be exactly as it wants to be.

Let it take you wherever you need to go next in your journey of awakening.

Trust that in every moment, you are always having the experience you are meant to have.

The experience you *need* to have -- or it wouldn't be happening.

And all of it is a part of your awakening.

If you seem unable to *experience* a process, *imagine* that you are.

Either way, your awareness expands.

Awakening is not a race, and there is no finish line to reach before anyone else gets there.

We're all in this together.

Whatever one of us realizes immediately becomes easier for the rest of us to become aware of.

Like flowers in a garden, each of us blooms when we're ready.

When we reach the moment when it is time to blossom, nothing can stop that from happening.

# PART ONE

✣ ✣ ✣

# The Essence
# of Awakening

✣ ✣ ✣

# 1

# The Story

On a beautiful spring morning in 1989 on the island of Kauai, tropical birds chatter in the lush foliage outside the Hindu Temple.

In the distance, a waterfall tumbles into a small lake.

As they quietly saunter toward the temple, two orange-robed monks pause to survey the idyllic scene from the stone walkway far above.

The tall, wide wooden temple doors stand open to the day's freshness.

Inside, it is an auspicious morning to be present for the Sunday service.

A monk announces that Gurudeva, the spiritual leader of the community, is forsaking his customary silent retreat to join the gathering.

He will soon be with us, the monk continues.

Not only that, the monk adds, he will give a talk.

This is a rare and welcome blessing.

Those assembled in the ceremonial room sit on the carpet in silence, preparing themselves to receive the words of this esteemed elder.

Several saffron-robed monks precede the holy man into the room.

At last Gurudeva appears.

With his white hair swept up in a bun and a luxuriant beard cascading down the front of his robe, he resembles a cross between an aging hippie and a cosmic Santa Claus.

His rosy cheeks crinkle as he smiles delightedly and seats himself before us.

Gurudeva's words are elegantly simple.

"We are all radiant beings of light," he begins.

"Our essence is light -- the limitless light of God.

"Our only problem is that we have covered up our light with so many 'overcoats' that our true nature is hidden."

He pauses to let us take this in and consider it.

The holy.man continues, "We don't need to fix ourselves -- we were never broken.

"There is nothing to change about ourselves, either, and nothing to add.

"Since we are all parts of God, who we are is already enough."

Gurudeva hesitates again to allow us to absorb his words.

Then he delivers the punch line.

"All we need to do is take off our overcoats!"

# 2

# Can Awakening Really Be This Simple?

Gurudeva's spiritual credentials were impeccable.

And his message was as simple as it gets.

We might paraphrase it like this:

*Who we really are is perfect,*

*since our essence is one with the Divine.*

*Our only task in life*

*is to release everything that obscures our inner radiance,*

*so it can shine forth in its full splendor.*

Can awakening really be that simple?

The short answer is *Yes, it can.*

So far, though, most human beings have not found awakening to be so easy.

That's because the human mind can find a million ways to make anything difficult.

3

Including awakening!

Minds like to think that waking up is inevitably a long, drawn-out process — a far-off goal that takes years, if not lifetimes, to reach.

Many people believe the true Self is an elusive, mysterious Something that requires great wisdom and massive effort to find.

Throughout history, humans have devised countless paths to awakening, with complicated practices and disciplines requiring decades to master.

Each path has its thick tomes to be read and absorbed.

All of this can keep us so busy that there is little time left to actually experience **being awake**.

This book is for those who are ready for a different approach.

It has been written with love for those who feel compelled to experience awakening **now** — not decades, or lifetimes, from now.

## The Radical Simplicity of Awakening

There are really only two things that are ever going on in our experience.

There is who we really are, and there is everything else.

In every moment, one of two things is happening.

We are resting in the joy, peace, love, and happiness of the true Self.

Or we are consumed by painful fears, thoughts, feelings, judgments, comparisons, and memories.

In short, we are either aware of who we really are, or we are suffering.

We are either peacefully, happily living as a soul in the human experience, or we are caught in our "stuff."

We suffer when we buy into our "stuff" and think it is real.

We suffer even more when we conclude that our "stuff" is who we are.

This is the bubble of Self-forgetting most humans live within.

We can buy new cars and get new jobs and trade one partner for the next, but the only thing that will ever burst this bubble of illusion is awakening.

Awakening is the way we discover true joy, happiness and love.

And awakening is not "out there" somewhere in an unknown future.

Awakening is happening now, and now, and now.

## Just Let Go

You are here to live as the magnificent manifestation of the Divine you came to Earth to be.

To increase the chances of living as a radiant soul, it helps to become familiar with your overcoats.

Then you can choose whether you'd like to keep them, or let them go.

If you decide that living life unencumbered by overcoats sounds appealing, you may want to become an overcoat removal specialist.

Shedding the overcoats that hide our light does not have to be hard work.

They fall away as gently as autumn leaves, once they are seen and accepted -- once we stop resisting them and making them "wrong" or "bad."

We do not need to judge our overcoats -- just love them and let them go.

We do not need to deny them, hide them, or tussle with them.

We can simply let them fall away.

Once we decide we would rather experience life in a lighter, freer way, we can't wait to release the excess baggage we have been carrying around.

We remove our veils and put down our burdens and soon find that life is a lot more joyful than we ever imagined it could be.

Our evolutionary edge is always the overcoats that are ready to be shed now.

They consist of whatever we have not yet been able to fully accept and allow.

Our overcoats contain all that love has not yet embraced — in ourselves and our life experience.

That can include uncomfortable body-sensations, painful emotions, limiting beliefs, fears, judgments, and upsetting memories.

Overcoats veil the ever-present truth of our luminous, divine nature.

We cling to them when we believe they are real, instead of seeing them as the disguises they really are.

Then we judge, deny, and hide them.

In the process, we accumulate *more* overcoats!

We fear our overcoats and suffer because we believe they are real and true.
But we don't have to be afraid of them.

And we don't need to judge ourselves for having them.

All we have to do is accept them and meet them with love.

## The Magical Power of Love

As a child, did you ever decide it wasn't safe to look under the bed, because you believed a scary monster lived there?

At some point, a helpful adult supported you in facing your fear.

Or you grew old enough or bold enough to challenge it on your own.

You gathered your courage — and a big flashlight — and soon discovered there was nothing there.

Facing our overcoats is a lot like that.

As we decide to love them instead of reject them, we love ourselves and stop rejecting who we are.

Bringing love to our overcoats makes it okay that they are there.

When we love whatever we come across, we feel relaxed with ourselves, just as we are.

As we bring love to anything and everything that shows up in our journey of awakening, everything within us softens.

Before we discovered that we could love our overcoats, we wanted them gone -- right away!

Their very presence seemed to say something negative and shameful about ourselves.

Now, having decided to love whatever we find, we are no longer so concerned about whether our overcoats drop away or stay put.

We know we are lovable in either case.

That relaxed, accepting attitude is exactly what allows overcoats to fall away.

7

When we are no longer fighting with what we come upon, we have stopped resisting it.

Now, we know there is no need to hide or deny our overcoats, or to frantically try to tear them away.

Once they receive our loving embrace, they have no reason to continue to burden us.

Then they easily and gently dissolve.

Love reveals the fact that they never really existed.

There was nothing solid or true about them — it only seemed that way.

As the veils of illusion fall away, the light of the true Self streams forth.

This is who we really are, and now that light can guide our way.

Taking off overcoats teaches us that love is not something we do — it is who and what we are.

We become able to accept and even welcome whatever appears on the path before us, moment to moment.

*Ah, here is another overcoat*, we say to ourselves.

*I'm glad you're here -- I want to get to know you.*

*Please tell me about yourself.*

The overcoat is one more place within us that is ready to receive our love and acceptance.

And we are happy to give it.

Each time we are able to meet an overcoat with a welcoming friendliness, it begins to loosen up even before we have investigated what lies within it.

And we remember that beneath and beyond whatever we are experiencing, there lives a sacred core of light and peace that we can return to whenever we like.

For that is our true nature.

That is who we really are.

# 3

# What Awakening Is — and Isn't

Awakening is remembering who we really are.

It is realizing that we are far more than the limited, separated, and isolated human beings we seem to be.

Awakening lets us know that we are each part of Something Larger.

It doesn't matter what we call that Larger Beingness.

What matters is knowing we are a part of That.

As we awaken, we let go of all that we are not, so that we can live as who we are.

At first we believe we are who we are not more than we remember who we truly are.

The suffering that human beings experience arises from believing we are less than we really are.

As awakening progresses, we increasingly remember our true nature and live as the Self, not our overcoats.

Suffering decreases, while joy, peace, love, and happiness increase.

We were never meant to suffer through this earthly life.

We are here to live as the incandescent beings of light, love and life that we truly are.

When we forget who we really are, we suffer.

When we remember, we feel happy and at peace with ourselves.

Can awakening really be that simple?

Yes!

When we know awakening does not need to be complicated, it happens as gently and effortlessly as the unfurling of a rose.

## What Awakening is Not

Awakening is not about seeking or finding, striving or trying.

Awakening is not about getting someplace.

It is not about becoming a better version of ourselves.

It is not about fixing ourselves or changing who we are.

It is not about acquiring something we don't already have.

It is not about adding onto or becoming more than we are.

We do not have to exhaust ourselves in the effort to awaken.

In truth, awakening can happen without any effort at all.

# 4

# Are Overcoats Inevitable?

Each of us is a Self, here to radiate our light into this world.

As eternal souls temporarily visiting Earth, our light has become obscured beneath layers of thoughts and feelings and traumatic memories.

Our bodies have slipped from being the light-filled temples of our souls into distorted, diseased forms that can make living painfully difficult.

Does it have to be this way?

Or is there another possibility?

## How Awakened Beings Live

Awakened beings experience life in a very different way from most humans.

They tend to let whatever is happening be what it is, rather than fighting with it or trying to make it be different.

They have little or no resistance to what is present.

Instead, they go with it.

If sadness is arising, they cry.

When they feel happy, they smile and laugh.

Just as those who are awake do not **resist** the difficulties of life, they also do not **cling** to the happy moments.

Instead, they allow the full range of whatever comes next in the steady stream of experiences that we call human existence.

They know that experiences come and go, and there is no point in trying to hang on to them.

Awakened beings live a lot like small children do.

They exist in the eternal now.

Such beings feel what is there to be felt in this moment, and in the next moment something new happens.

Since each emotion or sensation has been fully experienced, it does not accumulate within them, waiting to be felt.

Instead, it naturally passes right through.

There is no grasping, and no rejecting.

No pulling anything in, and no pushing it away.

No wishing something different were happening.

Awakened beings, like all of us, have preferences.

But they are not ruled or constrained by them.

Such beings experience life as if they were flow-through teabags.

Nothing gets stuck; nothing stops the flow of experiences and emotions.

None of it has any reason to pile up as layers of overcoats.

Awakened ones move lightly through life, free and unencumbered.

Their passage through the day resembles a free-form tai chi dance.

We can never quite guess what interesting, unexpected move will happen next.

## Saying YES to What Is

In this human life, becoming enshrouded in overcoats is a nearly universal experience.

But in truth, it is always optional.

It happens to us when we forget who and what we really are.

As we remember — as we awaken to our true identity — we accumulate far fewer overcoats.

Awakening helps us to say YES to what arises, within and without.

We meet whatever is present with love and awareness.

We have no reason to defend ourselves against what is there, or to wish it were otherwise.

When we know who we are, everything that happens is seen as part of the passing show.

It has nothing to do with our infinite, eternal, true nature.

Why not let it pass by, like a cloud in the sky?

# 5

# Self and Not-Self

The Hindu teacher Gurudeva's story reminds us that beneath the layers of overcoats every human being is wearing shines the light of the Divine.

This is the radiance of who we really are -- the light of the true Self.

In daily life, how do we know if we are dealing with an overcoat, or experiencing the true Self?

If an underlying feeling of peace and contentment is present, we are at rest in the Self.

If challenging emotions or discordant thoughts arise, we are in the thrall of our overcoats.

Caught up in the veils of illusion, we have probably forgotten the Self that we truly are.

In our forgetting, we believe what the voices of the overcoats are saying.

As soon as this happens, suffering replaces our inherent state of reasonless happiness and peace.

We all intuitively sense the presence of our overcoats.

They feel inharmonious, burdensome, and restrictive.

The discomfort we feel beneath the weight of our over-coats can manifest as physical, emotional, and mental dis-ease.

Many people use the word **ego** to talk about that which is not of the true Self.

The term **ego,** though, has become loaded with judgmental overlays that can get in the way of understanding and acceptance.

Ultimately, like everything that is not who we truly are, the ego is an illusion.

At the level of absolute truth or reality, it doesn't even exist.

In this book, instead of discussing the ego, we'll stick with talking about overcoats.

It helps to remember that they are no more real than the ego is.

That's why, rather than spending endless hours hearing their stories and getting entangled within their layers, we will simply focus on two things:

**1) Being with and bringing love to whatever is present within the overcoats.**

**2) Remembering that not one overcoat has anything to do with who and what we really are.**

We don't have to have a clue about what to do with our overcoats.

As long as we are willing to acknowledge an overcoat's presence in our experience, we can trust that we will be taken on the journey that will help us to love whatever we find, release the overcoat and go free.

Just as the true Self is one-stop shopping for everything we really want in life, seeing everything else as an overcoat is a simple way to return to basics.

There are really only two things that are ever present in our awareness -- the radiance of our true Self, and everything else.

Seeing whatever else is going on as overcoats cuts through the complexity and reminds us to return to the fundamental steps that help our overcoats fall away.

The rest of this book will lay out those steps.

To begin the journey, the following Experience will introduce you to both your overcoats and your true nature.

## Experience: Inner Radiance and Overcoats

Remember to <u>download your free mp3s of the experiences at https://www.luminousself.com/taking-off-overcoats-experiences.html</u>

PART ONE: Your Inner Radiance

Set aside some quiet, undisturbed time and space.

Read these directions now, and refer back to them as needed during the Experience.

Let your eyes close, and become aware of your breathing.

Feel each breath coming in and going back out of your body.

Rest in the stillness and simplicity of doing nothing.

Open to the possibility of experiencing yourself in a new way.

Take a few moments to contemplate Gurudeva's discourse.

You might like to go back and reread the story in Chapter One.

Here is the essence of Gurudeva's teaching:

"We are really radiant beings of light," he stated.

"Our only problem is that we are wearing layers of over-coats that hide that light."

Become aware of any responses or reactions to his words that arose in you when you read them.

Notice if any of those responses are present right now.

Also be aware of any new aspects of your experience. You don't need to do anything about them — just notice whatever is present.

If what Gurudeva said is true, then right now, in your in-nermost core, shines the light of the Divine.

That light is within you all the time, or your body would not have life.

The spark of the One within you is beating your heart and pumping blood throughout your body.

It is drawing breath into your lungs and conducting all oth-er bodily functions.

Now, invite the radiance in the center of your being to come into your awareness.

Many people find that it lives just above their hearts, deep within the chest.

You may be able to sense, feel, or see the inner light at your core.

It might appear as a flame, a glow, or some other form of radiance.

Even if you cannot sense or see it, it is there.

Imagine it, or simply remember that it is there within you, even if you are not perceiving it right now.

You might also call the light forth -- invite it to come into your awareness.

Allow a few moments to be with whatever is occurring.

Let the awareness of your inner light go on for as long as you like.

There is nothing more powerful you can do to heighten awakening than basking in the light of who you truly are.

PART TWO: Your Overcoats

Now, turn your attention to your overcoats.

These are all the things that make it hard to sense and remember the divine light within you.

Although the word "overcoats" brings to mind outer garments, our overcoats are actually within us.

They include everything that hides our innermost divine nature.

Often, the first overcoats we become aware of are uncomfortable bodily sensations.

See if any of those are present.

Other overcoats may consist of painful feelings, tormenting thoughts, and harsh judgments about ourselves and others.

When we have buried our feelings from traumatic past events, they become overcoats we wear until we can bring love and forgiveness to what happened.

For the next few minutes, simply become aware of some of the overcoats you are wearing.

Invite the overcoats you are ready to see and know about to reveal themselves to you.

Let this go on for a long as it feels comfortable.

PART THREE: Self and Overcoats

Now, while you continue to be aware of the overcoats, also become aware of the radiant light at your core.

The light may be faint or very small, but it is there within you.

The light is there, and so are the overcoats.

At the right time, each overcoat will come off, revealing more of the light that is your true nature.

Overcoats are not bad or wrong.

They are nothing to be ashamed of.

They are merely layers of who we are not that are hiding the brilliance of who we are.

We have clung to these garments, thinking they were all we had, not realizing the magnificence that lies beneath them.

Our overcoats fall away as we bring awareness and love to them.

When each overcoat has received the attention and acceptance it needs from us, it no longer has a reason to exist.

When we can love ourselves even with our overcoats, sooner or later they drop away.

And until that happens, we can go on loving ourselves, overcoats and all.

## Reflection:

What was it like to become aware of the light at your core, while also being aware of your overcoats?

Was this a new way of experiencing yourself?

You might like to journal about this.

## A LOVING NOTE TO THOSE WHO BELIEVE THEY ARE "FAILING" AT THIS:

If it was difficult for you to "see" or feel the radiance of your true Self, begin by **envisioning** it.

And if getting in touch with your overcoats did not happen, simply **imagine** their presence and what they might contain.

Neuroscience reminds us that visualizing ourselves doing something stimulates the same regions of the brain as actually doing it.

Many athletes find this practice results in substantial improvements in their performance.

If you are getting frustrated and thinking of quitting, try it.

Ask yourself, *If I* **were** *"seeing" or feeling this, what would it look or feel like?*

After a while, imagination will segue into actual experience.

Traveling into your inner world over time invites the innate, higher-sensory capacities of the soul to come forth.

As overcoats of "*I don't know how to do this*" drop away, you will increasingly "see" and experience the nonphysical levels of reality.

These are the domains in which the soul lives.

Remember, when it comes to our inner world, notions of "failing" and "succeeding" are irrelevant.

Whatever you are experiencing is not good or bad, right or wrong.

It is what it is.

And it must be the very best it can be right now, or something else would be happening.

Decide to love and embrace it, just as it is.

Where you are in your journey of awakening is not something that can be graded or compared.

We are each exactly where we need to be.

If we could be "further along," we would be.

Sooner or later, we realize there is no such thing as "further along."

Every journey into full awakening is unique, and the way it unfolds can be nothing other than perfect for the being who is awakening.

Overcoats do not tend to peel away merely through reading about what helps that happen.

What works best is to put what you are reading into practice.

Allow plenty of time for the Experiences in this book.

They provide an experiential immersion in the concepts presented, so that you can live into them and make them yours.

Step by step, you will be led through the process of bringing awareness to your overcoats.

As you become familiar with the process and put it to use, you become an overcoat removal specialist.

And as the overcoats fall away, you will more and more fully know yourself to be the radiant light at your core.

That awareness has the power to completely change your experience of yourself and your life.

# 6

# Overcoats R Us — Or Are They?

If awakening can be simple, straightforward and effort-less, and if being awake is how we were meant to experience life, then why aren't we all walking around in the joy and peace of the awakened state?

Well, the truth is, we **are**, but we don't know it.

Our overcoats hide the ever-present reality of our true nature.

But who we really are never goes anywhere.

As Gurudeva's discourse reminds us, at our core we are always and forever radiant beings of light.

Our task as awakening humans is to remember the light that we are and let go of everything in the way of living as That.

If it's that simple, why aren't we all flinging off our over-coats in joyful abandon?

**Because we think our overcoats are who we are.**

We humans tend to become mesmerized by the mes-sages our overcoats unceasingly blare out.

Believing what our overcoats insist is true, we convince ourselves that our lot in life is fear, sickness, lack and limitation.

*That's the way it is, we tell ourselves.*

*That's who I am -- someone who suffers.*

This mistaken identity takes as many forms as there are human beings.

Examples:

Josh wears thick, scratchy overcoats of feeling burdened by life. When things don't go his way, he shrugs in resignation, muttering, "That's how life is."

Brad was an academic superstar in college, and his sense of self-worth is tied up with his grade-point average. His overcoats broadcast, "Look how good I am at everything!"

Elaine clings to her shabby, "poor me" overcoat of victimization. Her energy is chronically flattened beneath its weight.

Our core beliefs form our identities, the cumbersome overcoats that make it hard, if not impossible, to see that life could be any other way.

Deep down inside, many of us carry core beliefs and judgments like these:

"I'm bad."

"There must be something wrong with me."

"I am unlovable."

"I don't deserve good things to happen to me."

If any of the above descriptions sound familiar, you have just spotted one or more of your overcoats.

These layers of who we are not have a way of outpicturing in our lives, until we realize they have nothing to do with who we truly are.

As we awaken to this fundamental truth, overcoats drop away and the suffering they set in motion vanishes along with them.

## The Amnesia of 3-D

How did we get so confused?

To see our way through this, we need to adopt a larger perspective.

We need to consider our evolution as souls in the human experience.

Here is the scenario that makes the most sense to us:

Each of us, as a soul, chose to come to Earth to experience things that are only possible here, on a third-dimensional planet.

When we stepped into these human forms, we became entranced by the rich, sensory world of 3-D.

We got so caught up with all that goes on here that we identified with our bodily forms.

We believed our humanness was who we were.

We went to sleep to our larger nature and forgot how vast we really are.

In our amnesia, we lost touch with the larger Oneness, as well as the divine light at our core.

Forgetting that we are all part of one boundless Whole, we bought into the illusion that we exist separate and apart from one another.

And no wonder — this is the way things appear in 3-D.

"I" seem to be over here, while "you" appear to be over there.

Those who are heavily identified with this dimension would never even question this, for the outer appearance of things is very convincing when we have forgotten that any other level of reality exists.

Entranced by appearances, we found ourselves living on the surface of our being, forgetting there was anything deeper.

Before we knew what had happened, we were caught in webs of illusion and confusion.

We no longer had any idea who we were, or how magnificent our true nature was.

Most of us have spent lifetimes shrouded in veils of forgetting.

Asleep to our fundamental oneness, we have played many roles in the human drama of duality — victim/perpetrator, rich/poor, success/failure, loved/loveless.

## Awakening Out of Our Amnesia

Finally, the moment arrives when we lose interest in playing yet another role.

We no longer find ourselves fascinated by the human drama.

Deep within, we intuit that it is possible to go beyond the suffering of the human experience.

We reach the point at which the only thing left is to awaken.

What we want more than anything is to remember who we really are, beneath all the roles and costumes.

To step out of the play of duality and return to the oneness at our core.

When that time arrives, our journey through life goes through a fundamental transformation.

Now, we are no longer simply gathering experiences.

From this moment forward, all that unfolds can become part of the process of awakening.

Sooner or later, we come to trust that whatever is happening must be necessary to our awakening, or it would not be present in our lives.

Rather than resisting What Is, we embrace it, and invite it to show us what it has come into our experience to reveal.

Instead of sticking to our small, limited ideas about ourselves, we let them go and open to the larger truth about who and what we really are.

When we are sincere about awakening, Life showers us with all the help we need.

Whatever is important to see and know will be brought into our awareness so that we cannot miss it.

As we let go of the mistaken beliefs about who we are and what is possible for us to experience, the radiance of our innermost nature shines forth more and more fully.

Eventually, that light out-radiates all erroneous ideas and identities.

All that we endured in our forgetting eventually brings us to this shining moment.

Not one bit of it was wasted or beside the point.

We can bless the journey, for it has carried us into this present moment.

Now, we begin to know ourselves as the beings of light we truly are.

# PART TWO

✣ ✣ ✣

# The Foundations
# of Awakening

✣ ✣ ✣

# 7

# Opening to the Divine

*Oh, grant me my prayer that I never lose*
*the bliss of the touch of the one*
*in the play of the many.*

Rabindranath Tagore

*Gitanjali*

Before awakening, we experience ourselves as isolated, separate human beings.

We may feel as though we are alone and adrift on an unfriendly sea, with no life-raft in sight.

*How could there be a God?* we might wonder.

*There is so much pain and suffering here.*

*God wouldn't let this happen.*

When we are asleep in the dream of human life, the Universe appears to be a chaotic realm in which nothing but random, meaningless events unfold.

Suffering arises when we believe ideas like *Life is hard — that's just the way it is. There is nothing I can do about it.*

As we awaken, we realize we are part of something larger.

We begin to fathom that we do not exist in isolation from every other being.

We start to see that are all woven together in some mysterious way in which not one iota in Creation is left out.

Sooner or later we conclude that this intricate interconnectedness cannot be random happenstance.

There must be something infusing it all and holding it together.

Something far beyond the capacity of our limited minds to comprehend.

Throughout history, humans have given many names to the invisible something that animates and suffuses the web of life.

Some of us simply call it the Divine.

Other ways of referring to it include:

Infinite Intelligence

The Creator

Great Spirit

Source

All That Is

God/Goddess

The All in All

A Higher Power

Life

The Great Mystery

Many of us have our own way of referring to the larger something we sense is holding us and our life.

The term we use is not important, as long as it conveys the awe and wonder we feel.

Words can never fully transmit our amazement as we recognize that everything in Creation is a manifestation of the Limitless Something.

But words will have to suffice until we all become telepathic.

So we will use words, knowing they are inadequate to fully express the inexpressible.

For some, the word *God* feels insufficient to impart the grandeur of the Divine.

The word *God* also has negative religious connotations for many of us.

For these reasons, a variety of terms for the Divine will be used throughout this book.

Feel free to substitute your own favorite way of referring to the Limitless One if you don't find it here.

## The Divine and Awakening

We do not have to know how to awaken.

Nor do we need to know how to remove our overcoats.

We do, however, need to be willing to ask Something Larger for help, every step of the way.

We need to humbly admit that we have no idea how to awaken ourselves.

And we may as well become comfortable with the reality that on our own, we do not have what it takes to awaken.

That requires far more of everything than our small human selves possess.

It is essential, then, to turn our awakening over to the Divine.

This guarantees that we will be taken through the exact life experiences that will help our overcoats to fall away, revealing the Self that we are.

When we open to receive divine assistance, we can trust that God will take off our overcoats in the perfect way and timing for us.

As overcoats peel away, the light at our core shines forth to bless the world.

Then, each of us lives as the radiant being we were always meant to be.

The Shining One we have always been, beneath our overcoats.

Now, we know what it is like to be a Buddha, a Krishna, or a Christ.

These were not special beings, in a class of their own.

They were just like us -- with one important distinction.

The only difference between them and us is that they awakened from their sleeping, human state and realized who they really were.

As Gurudeva might have put it, these beings shed all of their overcoats and walked the Earth free and unencumbered, fully awake and alive.

Once they awakened, they spent the rest of their lives living, creating, and expressing as the luminous Selves they knew themselves to be.

## Contemplation: The Divine and You

PART ONE: Your Attitudes Toward God

What does the word God evoke for you?

During your childhood, did you take on any negative or limiting imprints about God?

For instance, were you taught that God looked like an old, bearded white guy on a throne, judging and smiting?

Were you instilled with fear of God?

Does the thought of God bring up guilty, shameful feelings?

Would it be helpful to separate the Divine from what you were taught about God as a child?

How would you rather imagine and relate to God?

What would you call this larger beingness?

Can you envision a God of which you are a part?

How does it feel to contemplate something larger that is holding you, your life, and your journey of awakening?

PART TWO: Early Experiences of the Divine

Many of us had sacred experiences as children, but later forgot about them.

Some of us saw fairies, angels, or other non-physical beings.

Many of us felt a mystical oneness with nature.

A few of us awoke to see Jesus standing near the bed, or another holy figure taking form to give us solace and comfort during a challenging time.

As adults, we may have decided God was a figment of our imaginations.

Or we may experience the Divine as a living Presence in our lives.

In either case, after you've read these directions, let your awareness travel back to your childhood.

37

Can you remember a time when you knew you were a part of something larger?

Or a time when you felt the presence of something you can only refer to as divine?

Did you ever fall into a profound peace in which you knew that everything is perfect just as it is, despite outer appearances?

Invite your eyes to close and allow some time for memories to arise.

What were you feeling?

Were you alone, or with others?

Let yourself fully experience the sounds, smells, tastes, and feelings that were present.

Be aware of even the subtlest impressions in your awareness.

Notice if there are any parts of your body that come alive as you revisit this earlier time in your life.

As your experience feels complete, allow your eyes to gently open.

Notice what stays with you from your journey back in time.

You might like to continue to contemplate and journal about your immersion in the Divine.


## Reflection:

There is often a big difference between what we were taught about God and what we discover through our own living experiences of the Divine.

As we awaken, we nestle into the comfort of knowing that we rest within this greater beingness.

We are held by it, forever and ever.

We cannot fall through the cracks.

In fact, we realize there are no cracks!

Awakening reveals that everything is inextricably woven together within the Great Web of Life.

Including us.

As we come to know that we are forever held by Something Larger, overcoats of aloneness, isolation, and carrying the burden of our lives on our own fall away.

What remains is the deep peace of knowing we rest within a larger, all-inclusive beingness.

And just as we exist within this larger Whole, **it** lives within **us**.

# 8

# Sparks of God

*My Self is holy*
*beyond all the thoughts of holiness*
*of which I now conceive.*
*Its shimmering and perfect purity*
*is far more brilliant*
*than is any light that I have ever looked upon.*

*A Course in Miracles, lesson 252*

If it is true that beneath our overcoats shines the radiant light of who we really are, how did that light get there?

And where did it come from?

What is it that beats our heart and sends air in and out of our lungs?

Are our bodies simply an accumulation of mechanistic, biological processes?

Or is there something that shines out from our eyes that is beyond merely physical explanations?

Many of us turned away from God because the religious beliefs we grew up within felt confining and dogmatic.

The God we heard about in church didn't seem to have much to do with our daily lives.

As we awaken, we find ourselves reconsidering all that we learned and absorbed about God.

We may not have resonated with our religious upbringing, but we sense there is *something* beyond ourselves, even if we can't articulate much about it.

And this ineffable *something* seems to be at work not only in the stupendously enormous realms of galaxies and universes, but also in the microcosm of our own lives.

We can't help noticing that no matter how hard we try to orchestrate our lives, they go as they go.

However we attempt to control the unfoldment of events, they seem to have a life of their own.

Occasionally, we glimpse that our own little lives are a part of a much larger pattern.

We may even sense the Divine at play in the seemingly magical way connections are made and situations unexpectedly resolve.

This seems to be one of God's favorite ways to reveal Itself to us.

As we awaken to who we really are, we realize that God is not only somewhere above us in a heavenly realm, as we may have learned as children.

If the One animates all forms, then it must be animating our own form as well.

And the same intelligence and power and creativity and all other qualities of this Something that enlivens every living being are present within us.

In fact, they not only reside within us -- they **are** us, as our most fundamental nature.

At first, this may be merely an intellectual concept -- something we've read or heard.

It sounds good, and we want to believe it, but we haven't yet lived into it as a basic truth of our existence.

We may even question whether it could possibly be true since we seem to be so small, limited, and flawed.

As we awaken, we become aware of our true nature as a living reality, not merely a spiritual concept.

We are blessed with experiences that reveal, beyond all doubt, our essential identity.

Awakening means that our true nature is no longer just something we have read or heard about.

As we awaken, we come to *know* that there is an ineffable *something* that infuses and unites every living being in Creation, ourselves included.

We realize the Divine lives in us, just as we live in It.

That can only mean that we, ourselves, are as sacred and holy as the God we once believed lived "up there" someplace.

Whether gradually or all at once, this truth replaces all previous operating systems.

The next Experience provides an unusual way to experience your true identity.

Remember, if you are not finding yourself actually *experiencing* what is suggested, *imagine* that you are.

## Experience: A Drop in the Ocean, the Ocean in a Drop

PART ONE: Being the Ocean

Set aside some quiet time when you will not be disturbed.

Read these directions now, and refer back to them during the Experience as needed.

Become aware of your breathing, without trying to make it be a certain way.

Enjoy feeling each breath coming and going, just as it likes.

Now, imagine an endless ocean, stretching out in all directions.

See its color, feel the slight breeze rippling its surface, and sense the enormity of this vast body of water.

Merge your awareness with the ocean so that you **are** the ocean.

Feel the immensity of your depth and expanse.

Where your surface meets the air, swells rise up and fall away, but the ocean goes on being the ocean.

And as the ocean, you go on being you.

Countless individual drops make up your totality as the ocean.

You encompass them all; not one drop can possibly be left out of your vast wholeness.

Feel yourself as the sum total of all the drops.

Enjoy this contemplation for as long as it wants to continue.

PART TWO: Being a Drop in the Ocean

Now, bring your awareness to one of those drops.

It doesn't matter which one.

Become aware of yourself as this tiny drop within the seemingly limitless expanse of the ocean.

You exist within the amorphous whole of the ocean, yet you can also experience yourself as a distinct part of it.

Although you can feel yourself as a unique and particular drop, you can never completely separate yourself from the totality of the ocean.

That means that all that makes the ocean what it is lives within you.

The essence of the ocean is one with your own essence, since you are an inextricable part of the ocean's totality.

Float in the awareness of yourself as a drop in the ocean for as long as you like.

Now, transfer this experience to that of yourself as a human being.

You are a drop in the ocean of divinity, and all of the capacities and characteristics of the One are present within you.

All the possibilities of the Divine are inherent in your own true nature.

As an individual soul, you, along with all other souls, rest within the larger whole of the All in All.

Everything present within That is also present within you, waiting to be experienced and expressed.

You are a drop in the ocean, and the ocean in a single drop.

**Reflection:**

What was it like to be the entire ocean?

How did it feel to rest in the enormity of yourself as the entire body of water?

What was it like to be a drop within the all-encompassing immensity of the ocean?

How does this experience affect your perception of who and what you are?

# 9

# The Limitless Love, Intelligence, and Power of the One

*A man is the facade of a temple wherein all wisdom and all good abide.*
*What we commonly call man,*
*the eating, drinking, planting, counting man,*
*does not, as we know him, represent himself, but misrepresents himself.*
*Him we do not respect, but the soul, whose organ he is, would he let it appear through his action, would make our knees bend.*
*When it breathes through his intellect, it is genius;*
*when it breathes through his will, it is virtue;*
*when it flows through his affection, it is love...*
*All reform aims...to let the soul have its way through us.*

*Ralph Waldo Emerson*

Since God lives within us as our most essential Self, it only makes sense that we each contain everything the Divine Totality includes.

Every attribute we revere and worship in the Divine also lives in us.

We may not have *fully realized* these divine qualities -- we may not *live* them in every moment -- but they always exist within us, waiting to be discovered and ever more fully embodied.

In fact, many believe the journey through all our lifetimes has one central purpose: to live on Earth as the magnificent Divine Presence we truly are.

As we live our way into this lofty goal, we more and more fully radiate every divine quality out into the world.

We become beacons of harmony, peace, kindness, and all other attributes we see in our divine Source.

We admire these qualities in the Great Ones who have come to Earth to more fully anchor the Divine here.

In many spiritual traditions, three qualities are recognized as fundamental facets of the One.

They are Love, Intelligence, and Power.

All three attributes are present within each of us in varying amounts.

It is a rare human who expresses all three equally.

Such beings are often referred to as realized masters.

In most of us, one or two divine qualities are more fully experienced, while we may not feel as strong in a third.

Particular phases of our journey through life may focus on one or more of these primary attributes.

Perhaps early in life, intelligence was all-important.

Now it's all about strength and courage; a few years later, love moves to the forefront.

We may notice that our challenges give us opportunities to develop a quality more fully.

Life also has a way of putting us around others who embody the attributes we want to more fully incorporate.

Rather than idealizing such beings and putting ourselves down for our seeming deficiencies, we can recognize that they may have more fully integrated what we want more of.

At these moments, we can affirm, "That's for me!"

## Love

When our hearts are open, we feel love for ourselves, one another, and all beings.

We experience empathy and compassion for the struggles of humanity, whether our own or those of others.

We care about those less fortunate, along with the countless beings of all species who cannot act on their own behalf.

We want to help, to make a difference, to be of service.

When Divine Love is flowing through us, our energy feels safe and nurturing to others; we may find ourselves surrounded by those who need the loving-kindness we embody.

To the degree that the divine quality of love is alive and well in us, we seek out opportunities to share that love.

Gradually, we come to know that love is not something we **do** — love is the very fabric of what we **are**.

As our awareness of love expands, we recognize that love is the driving force in all of Creation.

Immersed in the sea of Divine Love, we see nothing but love in the outworking of the Divine Plan for our lives.

We know that even when things seem challenging, all is held with the endless, loving embrace of the One.

## Intelligence

When we look at the natural world, we can only marvel at the level of intelligence that created everything in existence, from the tiniest ant to a massive whale.

That intelligence not only set Creation in motion -- it sustains it continuously, every second of every day.

Divine Intelligence knows how to keep our heart beating and all bodily systems functioning, with a degree of intricate orchestration that is unfathomable to our human minds.

When we are in touch with this divine attribute, we feel confident that we can tap into the insight and guidance we need to handle our daily challenges.

We may enjoy stimulating our minds through reading and studying, solving puzzles, learning new things and playing challenging games.

The limitless creative intelligence of the One is alive in us, and we express it in a variety of ways.

We solve problems, think of solutions, manifest inventions and come up with work-arounds.

It can be tempting to believe that we are the originators of all of this, but in truth God's thoughts are pouring into and through our human brains.

The endless creative intelligence of the One combines with the unique energetic quality of our mental realm to produce ideas and accomplishments that have never been seen before.

Tapping into Infinite Intelligence, we delight in the "Aha" moments that let us know we are glimpsing a far vaster level of awareness than we usually experience.


## Power

Can any of us even begin to imagine the power it takes to keep galaxies spinning?

To move mountains, spew lava, or rearrange continents?

To thrust a green spear of life up through the frozen ground in spring?

When we feel Divine Power moving through us, we have no doubt that our will, in alignment with Divine Will, can accomplish whatever goals our soul deems worthy.

We may not lift weights for a living, but we sense a wellspring of strength and courage within us that will come forth as we need it.

We feel sturdy and competent and maybe even a bit indomitable from time to time.

Divine Power lets us dream big, knowing we will be able to manifest those dreams through sustained focus — and perhaps some hard work.

Accessing Divine Power, and sensing our will is in harmony with Divine Will, we do not take NO for an answer!

## Contemplation: Divine Love, Intelligence, and Power

As you read about the three primary divine qualities, you may already have identified which one or two are strongest in you.

You may also have determined which quality seems to be less developed at this point in your journey of awakening.

After you've read the directions for each attribute in turn, allow a few moments for your awareness to turn inward.

First, consider the divine quality of **love**.

How is this attribute manifesting in your life?

Allow images and memories and relationships to surface as they will.

Notice any emotions and thoughts that accompany them.

When you look within, does love seem to be a core aspect of your being?

Do others tend to view you as a loving person?

Are you satisfied with the amount of love that is present in your life?

Consider what has emerged from this brief contemplation.

And give yourself some love and appreciation right now.

Now, turn your awareness toward the attribute of **intelligence.**

In what ways does this divine quality express itself in your life?

Consider the entire course of this lifetime.

In what ways do you experience your awareness being filled with Divine Intelligence?

Do you ever find yourself suddenly filled with ideas, creative inspirations?

Do you sometimes know things that you have no earthly way of knowing?

Do others look to you for certain kinds of applied intelligence?

Does your life offer plenty of opportunities to express this divine quality?

Are there ways you would like to tap into Divine Intelligence more fully?

Finally, consider the attribute of **power.**

Do you see yourself as a strong, capable person?

Do you feel confident that you will be able to handle whatever arises?

Do others look to you for strength and draw upon your determination to persevere?

At times, do you feel an endless source of power flowing through you?

To what degree does your personal will influence your life and your world?

How fully and how often do you sense your will is in alignment with Divine Will?

Does your life contain sufficient outlets for your power?

In what ways would you like to express Divine Power more fully?

Which divine attribute seems to be the strongest in you at this time?

Is there one that you would like to experience more fully?

How might you experiment with that in your daily life?

# 10

# Surrender

*Surrendering yourself to God*
*is giving up what you really can't keep*
*in order to realize what you really can't lose.*

Shantideva

If everything in creation is an ever-unfolding expression of the Divine, then all that occurs in our journey of awakening is likewise held within the All in All.

Awakening, like everything else that goes on, is orchestrated by the Infinite Intelligence that knows exactly what we need to experience, every step of the way.

This means that we are not "doing" our awakening, any more than we are "doing" our lives.

We are not making awakening happen, any more than we are causing our hearts to beat or our lungs to breathe.

The idea that we cannot control our awakening flies in the face of much that our culture teaches.

From childhood, we are told to try hard, strive for success, and expend maximal effort to reach our goals and create the life of our dreams.

Even some so-called "spiritual" teachings insist that we can, and should, make our reality what we want it to be.

Some even suggest that our level of spiritual attainment can be measured by the extent of our material abundance.

"You can have it all," these teachings insist. "More is better."

While modern culture stresses that we can make ourselves and our lives into whatever we want them to be, awakening takes us in the exact opposite direction.

We find out that our little human selves cannot possibly know what would be best for us as souls in the human experience.

At the same time, we become aware that we rest within Something Larger that is infinitely intelligent and aware.

Wouldn't we want to invite that Something to direct our awakening process, if not our entire life?

If life is being lived through us, doesn't it make sense to invite That which lives in us to take the reins?

How could we possibly know, with our human minds, the best way for our awakening to unfold?

How can we even guess at what is in our best interest?

Fortunately, the infinite wisdom, power and love of the One Great Beingness are available to us in every moment.

Everything we need to awaken with the greatest ease and grace is just waiting for us to open to receive it.

All we need to do is ask.

In the Hindu tradition, those who worship the divine aspect called Shiva chant, "Om namaha shivaya" -- *I surrender to Shiva.*

They may prostrate themselves at the feet of an empowered statue or image of their deity, giving their lives to their God.

With the same sincerity, we can choose to surrender our lives to the Divine.

We can release control and take our hands off the steering wheel.

We can stop clinging to the belief that we know best, and choose to trust that God knows best.

Just as we admit we have no idea what is meant to happen in our lives, we can admit that we don't know the way to fully awaken.

We have no idea how to get from here to there.

If we did, wouldn't we already be there?

The fastest path Home to our true Self is to release our little human will and surrender to the will of God.

In the process, we will come up against the limits of countless beliefs and judgments about ourselves and our world.

For instance, we may discover that what looks like success to the world may, in fact, be a failure of nerve to live from the soul.

And what the world judges as failure may be viewed as absolute success through the eyes of the true Self.

How familiar are you with surrender?

The following Contemplation is designed to evoke your life experience with this cornerstone of awakening.

## Contemplation: Remembering a Time When You Surrendered

After you have read these directions, close your eyes and invite your awareness to travel within.

Ask to be brought back to a time when, despite your best efforts, you came to the limits of your human capabilities.

You felt utterly overwhelmed, afraid of what would happen next.

Whatever you faced was clearly beyond what you had to bring to it.

As you realized this, you had no choice but to let go.

You might have found yourself turning it all over to Something Larger, however you might have conceived of that and whatever you may have called it.

You may even have prayed for help from Beyond.

Remember what it felt like to give up -- to realize you didn't have what it took -- but it was OK, because you knew that larger Something was holding you and your life.

Let your memory travel forward in time to the outcome of this situation.

Can you see the Hand of the Divine in it?

How did God intercede and make Its presence known?

Did Infinite Intelligence move in ways your little human self could never have come up with?

You may have noticed synchronicities — meaningful, even magical events that could not possibly have happened by coincidence or chance.

How did the Divine resolve the situation?

Let yourself remain with this memory for as long as you like.

Savor the gifts of the experience.

You might enjoy writing about it in your journal or notebook.


## The Unending Spiral of Surrender

The pathway into full surrender does not travel in a straight line.

It spirals through our lives, always circling around to yet another opportunity to surrender.

At each turn of the spiral, we are a bit more ready and willing to turn it all over.

So we give it all to God — and then grab it all back. We get busy figuring out what to do and how to do it.

We lie awake at night wondering how we will ever manage, and then it comes to us: *Turn it over!*

So we surrender yet again, and rest in the peace of handing it over to God.

Until the next time our human self grabs the steering wheel.

Gradually, we remember more quickly to give our concerns to the Divine and ask to be shown the way through them.

This creates a new neural groove that deepens each time we remember to surrender.

Over time, the self-reinforcing loop of surrender takes over.

Turning it over to God becomes our habitual response to whatever arises.

We get less busy with the next thing that comes along, finding it much more relaxing to turn it over as soon as possible.

Surrender allows our life, and our awakening, to unfold with the ease and grace of a tree budding out in spring.

## Experience: Surrendering

The following inner experience contains three parts.

You may choose to do them one at a time with some open space in between, or all at once in a fiesta of surrender.

See what feels right to you and go with that.

## PART ONE: Surrendering an Issue or Challenge

Whether surrendering to the Divine is a new idea or a familiar response to life's challenges, there is always a new level of surrender available to us.

Take stock: Have you lived your life as though you were making it happen?

Or is surrendering to the Divine a frequent response to life's challenges?

Most of us probably fall somewhere in between.

Whatever your history with surrender, check inside to see if there is an issue or challenge you've been holding on to, trying to figure out, or worrying about late at night.

It doesn't have to be earth-shattering.

Let the issue rise to the surface of your awareness.

Get a good look at it.

Is it time to surrender it into the care of a larger level of reality that knows what to do with it?

There is no need to wait another moment.

Give it to the One Great Beingness, the source of all wisdom, love, and strength.

It can help to declare your intentions out loud.

You might find yourself saying something like, "God, I don't know what to do with this. But I know that You do. So here -- take it. Please show me the way through it as only You can."

Another prayer offers a simple way to surrender: "God, open the doors that need to be opened and close the doors that need to be closed."

This can refer to a specific question or life in general.

So right now, allow the words that are right for you to arise.

Make sure the words express your willingness to turn the issue over to the Divine.

And give thanks that Divine Help is available to you -- now and forever.

Once you have surrendered the issue to the Divine, notice how you feel.

See if any part of you is attempting to hold on to the challenge, believing it must find the way through on its own.

That, too, can be surrendered.

PART TWO: Surrendering Your Awakening

Have you believed you should know how to awaken?

And then admitted that you didn't have a clue about how to bring that about?

Have you ever thought you should be more awake than you seem to be?

Or judged yourself as a spiritual slacker, a failure at this mysterious thing called awakening?

Have you compared your "spiritual progress" to that of others and believed you came up short?

Well, relief is at hand.

If we are not living our lives -- if, in fact, Something Larger is living through us -- then that Ineffable Something must also hold our entire journey of awakening within Itself.

It, not our little human selves, must be orchestrating the unfoldment of not only flowers and universes, but also our process of waking up.

From our limited, human perspective, we can't know how our awakening would optimally unfold.

But something larger does.

And just as that Larger Something beats our heart and breathes us, It brings awakening about -- in the perfect way and timing for each one of us.

The same intelligence that regulates billions of incredibly complex life processes in the human body likewise stewards our awakening.

The unfathomable power that births galaxies allows us to triumph over even the most daunting challenges along our path.

The love that nourishes and sustains all forms of life, from the tiniest microbe to the largest cetaceans, impels and infuses every step in our awakening.

Without the infinite love, wisdom, and power of the Divine, we would not exist, much less awaken.

Realizing this, we can turn over everything about how and when and at what rate we awaken.

We can give it to the Infinite Intelligence that is managing it all.

"Not my will, but Thine."

This acknowledges that awakening is out of our own control and hands the process over to the Divine.

Allow a prayer of surrendering every aspect of your awakening to form itself within you.

Speak it aloud in the words that feel right.

Turn your awakening over to the One who knows how best to bring it about.

Relax about awakening and go free!

How does that feel?

When our judging, comparing overcoats grab hold of our awakening and we start to feel bad, we can remind ourselves to turn the process back over to the Divine.

These moments of lucidity go a long way toward reducing suffering so we can experience more ease and joy.

But there is an even more effective way to ensure that we are floating down the river of life in harmony with the journey rather than fighting to go upstream against the current.

It is possible to turn *our entire lives* over to God.

This affirms that it really isn't our little life anyway, but God's life.

Is today the day to surrender the whole of your existence to the Divine?

If now is the time, allow the words that are right for you to arise from within.

As you give them a voice, feel the deep relaxation of turning it **all** over to God.

Every bit of it!

What a relief — you don't need to have a clue about what to do with any of it!

How does this feel?

Enjoy your inner experience for as long as you like.

## Reflection:

PART ONE: Surrendering an Issue or Challenge

What was it like to surrender a current challenge to the Divine?

Did a part of you want to hang on to the issue, believing you should be able to find your own way through it?

How did it feel to choose to surrender it instead?

If the issue crops up again in the days ahead, repeat this process as necessary.

Remember to let the Divine orchestrate how it will be resolved.

In your journal, you might want to record what the issue was and when you first turned it over to God.

Every week or so, evaluate the situation. How has it shifted?

At some point, you will realize it has resolved, possibly in a way you would not have expected.

Often, the Divine handles our challenges so completely, we forget we even had a problem.

PART TWO: Surrendering Your Awakening

How did it feel to turn your awakening over to the Divine?

Did this change the way you view your journey of awakening?

If so, how?

PART THREE: Surrendering Your Life to the Divine

Was it time to turn your entire life over to God?

If so, what happened when you surrendered every aspect of your life to the Divine?

How do you feel now?

## Surrender: The All-Purpose Antidote

Awakening presents us again and again with a fundamental choice.

We can act as if we are in the driver's seat of our lives.

Or we can turn the steering wheel -- and our lives — over to the One who wants to live through us.

When the small, human self is behind the wheel, we feel inadequate to the task.

This is accurate, because we are.

We need levels of intelligence, power, and love far beyond what our little selves can ever manage to come up with.

When we cannot find what we need within ourselves, we look everywhere for those divine qualities, only to come up empty.

All addictive behaviors rest in this underlying search for something more.

We eat, drink, use substances, shop, work, travel, and do all kinds of other things to extremes, hoping to bolster our little selves so they can do what needs to be done.

But we will never find what we are truly seeking in any of these pursuits.

When we turn our lives over to the Divine, outward seeking gradually falls away.

We come to trust that our sacred core contains everything we need to live our lives.

When we know that, what need is there for addictive substances or compulsive pastimes?

As we rest in the comfort of knowing the Divine is living us, we trust that whatever unfolds next is a part of the larger pattern of our lives.

It will have meaning and purpose, because it is divinely orchestrated.

## Surrendering the Doer

Surrender is not a once-and-done thing.

As we come to see the wisdom in turning things over, we find ourselves surrendering many times a day.

What a relief to release our hold on our lives and allow Something Bigger to live through us!

At every stage of awakening, our ever-increasing faith and trust strengthen our willingness to surrender.

The more fully we surrender, the more easily we shed our overcoats.

Some of the heaviest overcoats accumulated from believing that we are in control of our lives -- believing that we make things happen.

Believing we are the Doer of our lives.

As we surrender, all the ways we've wrapped ourselves in the illusion that *we are doing our lives* unravel and fall away.

And we discover yet another gift of surrender.

 Surrender is the doorway to Grace.

# 11

# Grace

*Through many dangers, toils and snares*
*we have already come.*
*'Twas Grace that brought us safe thus far*
*and Grace will lead us home.*

"*Amazing Grace*"
*traditional spiritual*


If we are not awakening ourselves, if we are not "doing" our lives or our awakening, then how do we awaken?

We awaken through divine grace.

We awaken when it is time for us to awaken, and that timing is held in the larger pattern that encompasses each of our individual lives.

And we awaken in the ways that are right for us, ways that honor the nature of our soul-unfoldment over many lifetimes.

While we can learn how to help our overcoats fall away, we mustn't forget to acknowledge the role of divine grace in the process.

Through grace, the overcoats that obscure the light of our true Self dissolve.

Grace is the movement of the infinite love, wisdom and power of the One, always acting to awaken sleeping human beings.

Grace is forever looking for ways to lift us out of our amnesia and remind us of the fire of the Divine that lives in our core.

Through grace, our little human lives are brought into entrainment with larger cosmic forces.

As we surrender into this larger grace and know we are deserving of it, our awakening is expedited and hastened.

Grace means we do not need to effort at awakening.

Awakening will not happen faster through strenuous spiritual practices or austerities.

Hours of meditation each day will not hasten the process of awakening, unless this is the way the Divine is orchestrating our awakening.

And although many experience it as such and believe it must be so, awakening does not have to be hard or take a long time.

It does not require intense effort or acquiring reams of knowledge.

Through divine grace, awakening can happen as easily and beautifully as the unfurling of a rose.

## The Mysterious Ways of Grace

To our human selves, grace seems to be present during some times and absent at others.

Humans tend to believe grace is at work only when we deem what is happening "good."

We give thanks for the blessings, and pray for more grace — more "good" things — to pour in.

But grace is not limited to that which appears positive to our human preferences.

The more deeply we surrender into the Divine, the more aware we become that *everything* that happens in our lives is an action of Divine grace.

We realize that *whatever is going on* is the latest shower of grace watering our awakening.

It may seem mysterious and inscrutable to our human minds, but grace is always at work, no matter how things appear.

Whether our human selves see life events as "good" or "bad," we recognize that all of them can serve our awakening.

Realizing that *all is grace* deepens our surrender into Divine Will.

The greater our surrender, the greater our awareness of the grace that is continuously pouring into our lives.

## The Outworking of Grace

We all know what it feels like to experience the presence of grace.

We feel blessed, honored and exalted by Life Itself.

While we feel deeply grateful, an inpouring of grace may also cause us to become aware of overcoats of unworthiness.

We may feel unsure that we deserve the gift of grace.

But grace is not earned.

There is nothing we can do to become more deserving of its gifts.

Because we believe we must earn or be worthy of grace, most of us experience only a tiny trickle of the torrent of grace the Divine is continually pouring down upon us.

When we close down to and resist the movement of grace in our lives, we minimize the ways in which we can be blessed.

But as we come to see *everything* as grace in action, the miraculous outworkings of grace suffuse our lives with wonder.

We discover for ourselves the radical grace with which the Great Ones were on intimate terms.

As we awaken, we tap into the exalted, expanded grace that moved through way-showers like the Buddha, Krishna, and Jesus Christ.

These beings demonstrated possibilities we will one day all experience.

They were superconductors for divine grace.

And that grace emanated from them to bless others abundantly.

As each of us surrenders into the Divine, we, too, will find ourselves serving as conduits of grace.

Although expressions of grace can seem magical, mystical, and highly mysterious to our human selves, they are merely showing us how life can be.

There is nothing supernatural about what can happen through grace.

As the channels for grace open within us, we discover that grace is the normal, natural activity of the Divine manifesting Itself in our lives.

We know that we are not doing what happens.

As Jesus said, "I of my own self do nothing. The Father does all."

Knowing we do nothing other than make ourselves available, we feel humbly blessed to serve as agents of grace to express the Divine through our human forms.

In *The Mystical I,* Joel Goldsmith discusses grace.

When we know that the spirit of God lives within us, he says, we become children of God.

"Then," he promises, "you no longer live by effort, but by Grace. You then inherit your good. You do not labor for it, struggle for it, strive for it: you inherit it."

Knowing this, we declare to the Divine, "Thy grace is my sufficiency in all things."

## Contemplation: We All Experience Grace

Ask to be made aware of a time when you were aware of the presence of divine grace in your life.

It may have felt as if something magical happened, or a door mysteriously opened to something unexpected and wonderful.

You may have received an unexplained gift, or a release from a difficult situation that seemed to arrive out of nowhere.

Grace may have descended at a time when challenges were severe and you least expected anything good to happen.

Your awareness of receiving divine grace may have lasted but a moment, but that didn't diminish its impact.

Or you may have experienced a time of grace that went on for weeks, months, or even years.

Let yourself re-experience the sensations and feelings of that time.

What was it like?

You might like to write about your experience to re-kindle your awareness of what it is like to be in a state of grace.

And to invite that state to become your natural, ongoing way of being.

# 12

# The Power Of Love

*Whatever the question, love is the answer.*
*Whatever the problem, love is the answer.*
*Whatever the illness, love is the answer.*
*Whatever the pain, love is the answer.*
*Whatever the fear, love is the answer.*
*Love is always the answer because*
*Love is all there is.*

Gerald Jampolsky and Diane Cirincione
*Love is Letting Go of Fear*

Love has been called the Glue of Creation -- the force that holds it all together, the invisible essence that permeates and joins all beings.

Love unifies us all within the Divine.

As we awaken, we come to know that the Divine is synonymous with Infinite Love, and only wants what is best for us.

Seeing this, we more readily trust that whatever we are experiencing must be a necessary part of the process -- and therefore, a gift of grace.

No matter how it appears, and whatever its distressing disguise, it is present in our life for one reason only: to serve our awakening.

It has entered our world as an outworking of the infinite divine love that infuses everything in creation.

As we awaken to this reality, we penetrate below the level of outer appearances to the underlying substrate of everything in existence:

Love.

The Love of the One holds All within its neverending embrace.

It enfolds everything in Creation within its unfathomable caring and compassion.

This same flame of love burns within every one of us in our heart of hearts, as essential to who we truly are as air and water are to our human selves.

Just as God never met anything It couldn't love and accept, the love of the Divine within us finds nothing about us to reject or make wrong.

We do not need to earn this unfathomable love.

There is nothing we need to be or do to deserve it.

It flows into us and throughout all parts of our being in an effusive, unending stream, for this divine love is our birthright.

This love is what we are.

Our human selves judge, blame, and separate from everything about us that is less than our ideas and images of divine perfection.

But the Divine knows we are works in process, here on Earth to go through the challenges that will call forth more of who we really are.

All along the way, we will slough off the overcoats of human imperfection, revealing ever more of the divine truth of our beings.

As who we truly are comes forth, we find ourselves more able to love and accept ourselves, others, and whatever is going on.

We see the perfection in the imperfection and love it all, just as it is.

We are able to face and even embrace the overcoats yet to fall away, knowing they are not who we really are.

They are artifacts of the experiences we came here to endure and ultimately master, which are all part of the journey of awakening to the Self.

As we see our overcoats for what they are -- and what they are not -- we ever more easily love and accept ourselves, overcoats and all.

## Facing and Embracing our Overcoats

Awakening asks us to go beyond everything our overcoats are telling us.

When we are fully awake, we will experience life without any overcoats at all.

Awakening takes us beneath every one of them to the truth of who we really are.

As we awaken, we see that our overcoats have no ultimate truth, reality, or power.

When the love and light of consciousness penetrate them, they simply and easily dissolve.

They are like dreams created in our amnesia — the shadows cast by losing touch with the light of our divine essence.

On the way to fully remembering who we really are, we will have countless opportunities to bring awareness into the layers of what our overcoats contain.

We will also learn how to **face and embrace** what lies within our overcoats.

This may seem impossible to those of us who have spent years, or decades, avoiding or denying the contents of our overcoats.

Or judging them and making them — and ourselves — wrong, wrong, wrong.

We don't realize that we are the ones holding them in place with our fear of what they might contain.

The more we have walled ourselves off from them, the more we will need to slowly, gently, and lovingly invite our overcoats to reveal themselves to us.

Only when they have received our loving acceptance can they fall away.

For love is what each and every layer of our overcoats has wanted since it came into existence.

The first step is to **face** what is there within the layers of our overcoats.

To see it for what it is.

To stop running from our pain and suffering and decide to meet it with awareness.

The second step is to **embrace** whatever we find.

To wrap loving arms around the tormenting thoughts, relentless feelings, and obsessive fears.

To give ourselves empathy and compassion for the suffering we have endured.

To welcome every bit of it into the fold of our beingness.

It has been waiting for our embrace since the moment it originally layered itself within our overcoats.

When we can face and embrace what lies within our overcoats, they receive what they have always wanted.

As they are absorbed into the all-embracing love of the Self, our overcoats are effortlessly shredded.

They decompose and disintegrate within the universal solvent of love.

As our overcoats dissolve in that bath of love, the radiance of who we truly are comes forth more and more fully.

Facing and embracing our overcoats allows us to live more fully as the Self that we are.

This is the natural, inevitable process of awakening to the Self.

## Loving our Disguises

Lifetime after lifetime, we human beings have been wearing a myriad of disguises that hide the light that shines within us.

Life becomes very confusing when we believe our disguises are who we are.

We have identified with the costumes we are wearing instead of the essence of our being.

We may have thought we were a carpenter, a clerk, a diva, or a ditch-digger, when all along we are magnificent beings of light here to play yet another role on the stage of Earth-life.

Whether we wear the costume of someone who is lowly or grand, self-deprecating or arrogant, successful or an abject failure in the eyes of the world, beneath our disguise each of us has always been the same sacred emissary of the Divine.

Perhaps our souls wanted to try out a number of disguises over many lifetimes, to find out what each was like.

Wearing a variety of masks and veils allows us to experience a wealth of ways of being.

We couldn't get this breadth of experience in any other way.

As we gather into our Selves the knowledge and wisdom gained in each lifetime, we acquire empathy and compassion for the suffering of others.

We eventually realize that what we see them enduring was once our own travail.

Cultivating the ability to love despite our differences is central to why we are here.

Since our disguises play a vital role in this process, we can stop making them wrong.

There is nothing bad or shameful about them -- they are simply who we thought we were.

Like all of our overcoats, they are ultimately illusions.

Beneath the camouflage, we are what we are — souls, holy and whole aspects of the One.

As we come to know who we really are, and identify with That, we have no further need for disguises.

At that point, the veils peel off by themselves.

Once our masks receive the love and acceptance they have always wanted, they simply fall away.

There is nothing keeping them in place any longer.

And no one clutching and clinging to them, believing the overcoats are needed to protect us from a cold, cruel world.

Bathed in the warmth of love, our overcoats dissolve, revealing more of the unending divine love that is our true nature.

## Experience: Cultivating Divine Love

PART ONE: Opening to Love

For a few moments, contemplate your life as it is, right now.

Can you love yourself, just as you are?

Can you wrap whatever is going on in your life in an embrace of love?

Can you love yourself even if you are having trouble loving yourself?

Invite your eyes to close and continue to be with whatever is arising.

If you find it difficult or impossible to *love* yourself and what is going on in your life, see if you can simply *accept* yourself as you are.

When you have seen and felt whatever is within you, let your eyes open, and consider the following.

The more we deepen into who we really are, the easier it gets to love whatever is present.

Over time, our sense of who we are -- our identity -- shifts from the outer, human self to the inner, divine Self.

As we become established in the true Self, loving whatever is present in us and our experience gets easier and easier.

For love is the essence of the true Self.

Meanwhile, we can help this along with the following simple practice.

PART TWO: Seeing Through the Loving Eyes of the True Self

Become aware of a troubling aspect in yourself or your life.

See it through the eyes of your human self, as you have so many times before.

Hear the judgments.

There may be fault-finding of yourself, or of others.

Feel the frustration, fear and shame.

Notice the tendency to want to separate and move away from this distressing internal or external situation.

Just let it all be what it is, with no attempt to shy away from it, and no need to give it any energy.

Now, invite the eyes of your true Self to look upon the situation.

Invite the love of who you really are to bathe it in acceptance and compassion.

Let yourself feel what this is like.

If this seems challenging, invite the flow of divine love into the situation to increase.

How does the situation appear to your divine Self?

Allow some time for this new perspective to reveal itself.

If you don't immediately experience how your true Self would see things, then *imagine* how it would.

What do you now see and understand about the issue?

What is it like to feel divine love enfolding you and this challenging aspect of your life?

Knowing you are the Self, are you more able to love your human self through it?

PART THREE: Loving Ourselves as We Are

Fear and doubt and feeling bad about ourselves are clues that something in us is asking to be loved.

Not loved after it is healed, or transformed, or fixed, or gone beyond.

Loved as it is — as you are — **right now**.

The mind may come up with a zillion reasons why you are not deserving of love, why you are not worthy of your true Self's unconditional acceptance.

The reasons may sound convincing, and you may be tempted to side with your mind about the matter, but none of them is ultimately true.

To turn this around, try this.

Invite your mind to list some of its judgments and criticisms of you.

Don't engage with them — simply hear them out.

Write them down if that seems helpful.

Now, become aware of your breathing.

Notice the thoughts that are arising, and notice whether you are believing those thoughts.

Feel the emotions that are present.

Observe any guilt or shame stimulated by the mind's assessments of you.

Then turn everything over to the Divine, within and without.

Surrender it all into The One Great Being.

Now, ask to be made aware of how your true Self sees you.

Feel the vast love of who you really are enfolding your human self.

Sense the radiance that lives within you encircling all that is hard for your human self to accept and embrace.

Receive any loving messages that your true Self wants to communicate to your human self.

Allow some time to be with all that is unfolding.

Then write about your experience in your journal.

You can easily use this simple process in your daily life.

Whenever you notice the mind making a critical evaluation, stop.

Go through the steps presented above.

As you do this over time, the old neural groove of suffering will be replaced by a new response-pattern of self-acceptance and happiness.

Working with this simple practice reveals a profound truth:

If we can meet it with loving presence and awareness, every situation offers an evolutionary opportunity.

Each challenge that arises is another call to love.

Will we answer the call, or go on rejecting and judging our precious human self?

# 13

# Being Present with What Is

*The mystery of life*
*is not a problem to be solved,*
*but a reality to be experienced.*

*Aart van der Leeuw*

The first step in overcoat removal is to become aware that we are wearing them.

If we are experiencing anything other than the peace, love, joy, and wisdom of the true Self, we have encountered an overcoat.

This is a point of power, for now we face a fundamental choice.

Will we go toward the overcoat, or move away from it?

Will we pretend we haven't noticed it?

Will we block it out of our awareness with our consciousness-dulling "drug" of choice — eating, legal or illegal substances, shopping, or something else?

In other words, will we deny that it exists?

Or will we muster up the courage to begin to investigate the overcoat?

All we need to do is simply show up with the willingness to be with whatever reveals itself.

This is the path to freedom.

Some basic tools and processes can really help with this.

In the following chapters, you'll learn how to cultivate *conscious awareness*.

You can then bring your conscious awareness to whatever is present in your experience.

## Why Do We Run from Our Overcoats?

We may be afraid of what we will find in them.

We might fear we will be overwhelmed by them.

We might even believe that we **are** what our overcoats contain.

The fear of what we might find keeps us wanting to escape.

Fear causes us to run, to hide, to do anything but face what is going on within us.

Our culture constantly bombards us with messages that we should be consuming, checking our social media, or buying something — all of which are about looking "out there" instead of turning within.

In this outer-focused world, turning our awareness within is a radical act.

Many of our overcoats are woven through with compulsions, if not addictions.

These behaviors keep us from being present, right here in this moment, and experiencing what is happening within us.

They keep us endlessly distracted from who we really are and what is actually going on.

Since most of us are convinced we **are** our overcoats, we do not question the incessant thoughts that crowd our minds, or the turbulent emotions churning in our bellies.

We simply believe they are real and true — The Way It Is.

These thoughts and feelings act as veils that limit our perception of what is going on, right here, right now.

They prevent us from experiencing reality as it is.

This happens to us all, many times a day.

For instance, someone says something to us and we react based on what we think they said or the emotions that were triggered by their remarks.

We don't actually know or experience what really went on.

We are controlled by our mind and emotions.

Awakening is the process of freeing ourselves from this control, so that we can experience and respond to life from a deeper place within us, with the sacred awareness of the true Self.

## The Power of Presence

Awakening allows us to be fully present with the two fundamental aspects of our lives.

The first is **what is going on**.

The second is **what we are experiencing in relation to that**.

Most readers of this book will probably find themselves thinking, "I already do that."

Being present with What Is may seem so basic it is not worth mentioning.

But few human beings indeed have mastered the ability to fully meet with awareness what they are experiencing.

Since each of us is an inextricable part of the All in All, our consciousness and the consciousness of the One are, well, one.

When we are experiencing and witnessing whatever is arising *as it is,* without perceiving or interpreting through the filters of the mind, we are in the truth or reality consciousness of the Divine.

When we are fully present with What Is, the awakening, illumining consciousness of Source is acting through us.

We are seeing what is happening through the eyes of God.

The Divine doesn't need to do anything with what is present -- it just *is* with What Is.

When we bring consciousness to something, the illusions that have resulted from being unconscious and asleep begin to fall away.

This is the essence of awakening.

## Bringing Awareness to Overcoats

Overcoats are multi-layered, with all kinds of "stuff" mixed together -- feelings, sensations, ideas, images, stories.

Bringing consciousness to an overcoat means we are investigating it, from a place of curiosity.

Being with whatever reveals itself, layer by layer, begins to tease apart what has been glued together.

As the light of consciousness shines into the tangled webs of our overcoats, they begin to sort themselves out.

At first, we can feel so overwhelmed by these accumulated layers of "stuff" that we don't know where to begin.

But we don't need to know what to do or how to proceed, since we are not "doing" our awakening.

The Grace of the One knows what we need to experience next to release ourselves from our overcoats.

A helpful attitude to cultivate is to assume that whatever is present in our awareness is a gift from the Divine.

If that's the case, who are we to say no to it?

The outer appearance of an overcoat may be unpleasant.

Some overcoats are so distressing to look at, facing them full-on may seem impossible.

We'd rather do almost anything than be with what is there.

But the sooner we accept the overcoat, just as it is, the more quickly we can experience the awakening that lies hidden within and beneath it.

When we are willing to show up with whatever is present, God does the rest.

The One is perfect, omnipotent, and omniscient.

Infinite healing and awakening power, intelligence, and love are "doing" this journey of awakening.

As we awaken, we learn that we can completely trust the Divine with our awakening -- and our life.

## The Difference Between Pain and Suffering

Human beings often think and talk about pain and suffering as if they were one and the same.

Most of us believe this statement is true: *I have pain, therefore I suffer.*

Actually, we can experience pain without suffering one bit.

It is possible to be fully present with the mixture of sensations we label as pain, whether it is physical, emotional, or mental pain.

When we can do that, we do not suffer.

We merely experience pain.

87

It might be minor discomfort or full-on agony, but when we can be with it, pain is simply pain.

When we are *not* able to be with the pain, we suffer.

The mind may insist that something else should be happening.

Now we are caught up in judging what is present instead of being with it.

The more we give power to the thoughts and feelings that arise *about* the pain, the more we suffer.

We reduce suffering when we decide to be with whatever is happening.

We don't need to know what to do with any of it.

All we need to do is be with it.

That immediately begins to change our relationship to what is going on.

And quantum physics insists that the mere act of witnessing what is happening changes not only our relationship to it, but also *what is going on* itself.

Nothing stays the same when we are able to observe and be with what we are experiencing.

## What We Resist Persists; What We Face, We Can Embrace

Like life itself, awakening can progress easily, or with a great deal of resistance.

It all depends on how we greet the process each step of the way.

We can align ourselves with the fact that we are awakening, and view every experience we encounter as a catalyst for our awakening.

Or, we can resist what's happening and believe the thoughts that insist something else should be going on.

We resist what we are afraid of.

When resistance is happening, we probably believe the troubling thoughts and feelings that are present are real and true.

We might even believe they have power over us -- power to hurt us.

No wonder we don't want anything to do with them!

When we don't know how to welcome what is present in ourselves or our world, it can seem we have no choice but to resist it and hope it goes away.

Resisting what is present, though, only prolongs the process the Divine is orchestrating in Its infinite awareness of exactly what we need to experience at each moment of our awakening.

When we align with the Divine and ask It for help, the process of awakening is eased and expedited.

When we resist what the Divine is orchestrating and think we know better, we experience more suffering.

There would be no suffering if we didn't resist what was present.

Since we have been given free will, the choice is always ours.

Will we embrace or reject the next thing that happens?

# 14

# Our "Stuff" is Not IN the Way — It IS the Way

*As a human being related to all living beings*
*we must first be related to ourselves.*
*We cannot understand, love and welcome*
*others without first knowing and loving ourselves.*

Jean Klein
*Who Am I?*

During the early stages of awakening, we become aware that, as much as we might like to be, we are not living in the exalted state displayed by the Great Ones throughout human history.

Nor does our usual state resemble that of modern-day awakened beings.

Whereas they appear to be effortlessly happy and at peace, most of the time our mental-emotional condition is far from that untroubled equanimity.

We have to admit that, more often than not, we are consumed by our "stuff" — thoughts, feelings, judgments, relationship issues, and painful memories.

We don't want to be, but we are suffering.

Most humans embark on a spiritual path because they want to know how to relieve their suffering and be happy.

In this sense, our suffering is a blessing, for it encourages us to seek another way of being.

But all too often, we humans decide that our "stuff" — whatever it may be -- is in the way.

We find ourselves thinking, *If only I could get past this "stuff," I could really get somewhere spiritually.*

*If only this "stuff" weren't here, I could be happy.*

*This "stuff" is in my way. How can I get rid of it?*

But our rejecting attitude does nothing to relieve our suffering.

In fact, it intensifies it.

When we polarize against our "stuff" it becomes even harder to let go.

For, as we have seen, what we resist has a way of sticking around until it receives the love it has always wanted.

Our "stuff" not only sticks around, like a stray dog looking for love -- it actually **sticks to us**.

Our rejection of it glues it to us.

Remember the old saying, what we resist persists.


## How Could Our "Stuff" BE the Way?

Let's return for a moment to Gurudeva's teaching discourse.

This esteemed spiritual teacher reminded his listeners that we are radiant beings of light.

We don't remember that, he added, because we are wearing layers of overcoats that hide our inner light.

Gurudeva didn't make those overcoats wrong or bad.

He didn't judge anyone for having them, or shame anyone for hiding their light beneath them.

He merely said we need to take our overcoats off.

So how do we do that?

Our overcoats are composed of layer after layer of "stuff."

As we bring awareness to our overcoats, we are simultaneously getting to know more about our "stuff."

When we see it for what it is, and realize it has nothing to do with who we really are, the overcoats of our "stuff" easily and naturally fall away.

This automatically reveals more of the light that we are.

The more we identify as the Self, the more we remember that we **are** love.

The true, eternal Self has no problem loving our overcoats, exactly as they are.

And the Self likewise has no problem loving our little, human self, overcoats and all.

Receiving the love they have always wanted helps the layers of who we are not to drop off more easily and rapidly.

This self-reinforcing loop is core to the process of awakening.

The more we remember who we truly are, the less we identify with the "stuff" in our overcoats.

We accept that the "stuff" is there, but we don't give it any power.

As our overcoats full of "stuff" drop away, more of the brilliance of our true nature shines forth.

The more fully we awaken to who we are, the more we know that our "stuff" is not IN the way -- it IS the Way.

When we can meet our "stuff" with loving, accepting awareness, it shows us the Way into greater freedom and awakening.

Bringing loving awareness right into the core of the "stuff" invites it to do what it has always wanted to do.

As it reveals itself to us and receives the loving acceptance it has always wanted, the "stuff" goes through whatever process is needed to resolve it.

Then, it has no further reason to stay embedded within our overcoats.

It falls away as gently as the petals of a rose that has finished blossoming.

## Our "Stuff" About Awakening

Our overcoats are not only layered with "stuff" about ourselves and our lives, we also pile on overcoats about awakening.

They are made up of all the ideas we accept as true about the journey of awakening.

And the feelings and fears those ideas spawn in us.

Do any of these sound familiar?

*You can never stop seeking, or you won't awaken.*

*You have to work hard and even exhaust yourself to awaken.*

*There are so many spiritual books out there, I'll never have time to read them all, so how will I awaken?*

*I'm not sure I will be able to awaken. Do I have what it takes?*

*I'm too busy to awaken — I have too many Earth-plane responsibilities.*

Many awakening souls fear what they will have to let go along the way.

The fear may segue into terror as we contemplate the changes we believe awakening may ask of us.

We may have already glimpsed what the process of awakening can entail.

*It feels as though life as I've known it is ending. I have nothing solid to stand on anymore.*

*To awaken, you have to give up everything you love in life.*

*What will I lose if I get serious about awakening?*

*What will happen to my job? My home? My relationships? My way of life?*

*Will I have a social life? Or will everyone think I'm weird if I stay on this journey?*

*What about my standard of living -- will I have to live as a pauper?*

*Will I lose interest in the things I now enjoy?*

*What if life becomes deadly boring once I've awakened?*

*I'm not sure I would enjoy being quiet and peaceful all the time.*

Beliefs and judgments about ourselves may surface, too:

*I just don't have what it takes to awaken.*

*I have to try harder or I won't awaken.*

*I need to fix or change things about myself in order to awaken.*

*I need to get someplace other than where I am right now.*

*I'll have to show up all the time and I'm not sure I can do that.*

*I don't feel worthy of awakening. Why me? So many other people are more deserving of waking up than I am.*

Other overcoat voices judge how we believe our process of awakening is going.

*Everyone else seems to be awakening much faster than I am.*

*I have too much "stuff" in the way of awakening. I'll never get it all handled, so how can I ever awaken?*

*Awakening is for other people -- not me.*

*My friends see divine beings and nature spirits, but I don't. Maybe I should give up seeking awakening.*

*I'm a laggard, a spiritual failure.*

All of this "stuff" about awakening contains emotions we are probably not in touch with.

We may be too busy judging ourselves to remember to devote time to feeling what is present.

Instead of continuing to try and convict ourselves according to some illusory, impossible standard of spiritual success, we can give ourselves empathy and compassion.

We can face and embrace the feelings that arise, knowing they are part of the process of awakening or they would not be present.

We can also remind ourselves of some important truths:

It's OK to feel fear about awakening.

**In fact, it's OK to be terrified.**

This is new territory and we have no idea what lies ahead.

The normal, natural response to an unfamiliar situation often includes fear.

The presence of fear doesn't mean we are failing.

It simply means we are experiencing fear.

We can be with the fear and give ourselves love.

We can also appreciate ourselves for being willing to face and feel what is there within us.

Fear may arise at every new step along the way to full awakening.

Learning to be with fear -- without either shutting it down or giving it power — is an essential aspect of awakening.

Because this is so important, in this book you will find a lot of support for befriending, not rejecting, fear.

Chapter 19 is all about fear, and Chapter 34 includes a guided, inner Experience to support you in facing and embracing the fears you are experiencing, including fears about awakening.

## Accepting Our "Stuff"

Encountering our "stuff" about awakening is central to the process of releasing who we are not so we can live more fully as who we are.

We suffer when we tell ourselves, *This "stuff" shouldn't be here.*

Suffering stops when we accept the presence of whatever arises, knowing it would not be present if it weren't important to know about.

The more we can accept our "stuff" about awakening exactly as it is, the more fully we rest in loving ourselves.

And love is as awakened as it gets.

## Awakening is Fail-proof

Ultimately, none of us can fail at awakening.

And nothing -- including our "stuff," as we have seen -- can get in the way of our awakening.

In fact, everything that is going on -- now, and now, and now -- must be necessary to our awakening or it would not be present.

A caterpillar cannot fail to become a butterfly — it is built into its DNA to one day soar in absolute freedom.

And if you are a soul in the human experience at this time, it is your evolutionary imperative to awaken.

Remember, you are not doing this -- you are not awakening yourself, you are being awakened.

A larger beingness is guiding the process, not your small, human self.

Since you are not "doing" your awakening, you cannot get it wrong -- you cannot make a mistake.

You cannot get too caught up in your "stuff" and miss your opportunity to awaken.

For every new moment presents yet another chance for us all.

You are safe, and the process of awakening is safe.

You are going down a river, and the only question is whether you will let the current carry you or fight the current and make the journey more difficult.

On a river trip, we don't know what lies around the next bend until we are greeted by the murmuration of a flock of birds, a stunning vista, or a determined beaver adding branches to its dam.

In the same way, we can't know exactly how our "stuff" will turn out to be the Way to the Self.

But we can trust that if we agree to meet it with awareness and love, our "stuff" will show us the way Home.

For as we bring love and acceptance to the overcoats of our "stuff," they effortlessly peel away.

And what is revealed is the luminous radiance of who we truly are.

We have no idea of the joy that lies ahead, the gifts of grace we will discover, or the full scope of the Self that is just beginning to reveal itself to us.

But a powerful intuition of these possibilities is what keeps us going, even when the next rapids seem too scary to traverse.

Each of us will die and die again to who we thought we were and what we believed was possible.

And each time, out of the death and dissolution we will be reborn.

As the overcoats of who we never were fall away, the eternal brilliance of who we have always been shines forth more fully.

Each time, more of who we truly are will emerge from behind the veils that drop away.

At times awakening can feel like the most challenging thing we will ever experience.

We might yearn to remain asleep in our dream awhile longer, ensconced in our overcoats.

The mind's conveniently selective memory insists the dream was a sweet one.

Yet we also have to admit that it was permeated with suffering.

Once we find ourselves in the river of awakening, there is no turning back.

As scary and uncertain as it sometimes appears, we know this is the only journey worth taking.

And it is also the grandest adventure available to a soul in the human experience.

# 15

# No Truth, No Reality, No Power

*... the day before he passed away, he wrote me a note:*
*"This is all an elaborate hoax."*
*I asked him, "What's a hoax?"*
*And he was talking about this world, this place.*
*He said it was all an illusion.*

*Roger Ebert's wife, Chaz*

Who among us hasn't experienced getting caught up in our "stuff"?

It happens to us all from time to time.

It can even seem that our "stuff" is who we are.

We reinforce this illusion every time we say things like, "I am sick" or "I am disabled" or "I am an emotional wreck today."

Qualifying the sacred words I AM with anything other than the perfection of our divine nature leads us into limitation.

Now, we are no longer identified with our true magnificence.

Instead, we believe we are defined by the temporary challenges of the human condition.

Wrapped in the stifling overcoats of forgetting our true nature, we suffer.

In these moments, we need help from Beyond.

Fortunately, the Divine has provided a simple mantra that can instantly return us to sanity and remembrance.

Here it is:

**No truth, no reality, no power.**

The **truth** about us is that we are holy, pure, and perfect.

Anything other than that has no ultimate truth.

The only absolute **reality** is that God is, and we are part of That.

Everything else that is trying to pass itself off as real is an illusion.

Finally, the only true **power** in the Universe emanates from the Divine.

We humans unconsciously give power to all kinds of limited, distorted  ideas and conditions.

Because we are one with the Divine, our divinity empowers whatever we believe is real and true.

It's as if the Divine looks at what we believe and says, "OK, if you want to go with that, we'll energize it for you."

"Because you are a spark of the One, the same creative energy that manifests galaxies flows through you. You are a creator. If that's what you want to create in your life, go for it."

The power of the universe then pours into whatever we decide is real and true.

As those illusions are empowered, they can seem very solid and convincing to our human selves.

We then believe these overcoats of limitation have power over us.

We know we are caught in a web of delusion when we hear ourselves think or say, "That's just the way it is."

Do you hear the powerlessness in that statement?

We actually believe the false ideas embedded in our overcoats have more power than we do.

No wonder our limited, erroneous beliefs can have such devastating effects in our lives!

But ultimately, not one bit of it has any power at all.

It only seems that way because we have deemed it so.

All along the journey of awakening, we will be faced with yet another overcoat of who and what we are not.

Because our overcoats can seem so utterly real and true, we need a way to cut through the delusion and return to reality.

That's where the mantra comes in.

We stand firmly in the power of who we are when we can view whatever arises while remembering one simple fact:

**This has no truth, no reality, and no power.**

When "stuff" arises, this mantra reminds us we are dealing with illusion.

Even the heaviest, most oppressive "stuff" of our overcoats, the "stuff" that seems so real we have decided it is who we are, has no ultimate truth, reality, or power.

When a discordant thought or feeling arises, we can remind ourselves that, despite what our mind and emotions are telling us, nothing that denies the divinity of our Self and our Source can be true.

However real this experience may seem to be, it is not a manifestation of our true, divine nature, and therefore it has no power over us.

There is only one reality: we are holy, pure and perfect divine beings.

Anything that belies this has no ultimate reality.

As Gurudeva's story brings home, there is who we really are, and there is everything else — layer upon layer of the overcoats that hide our inner light.

The more often we remind ourselves that our overcoats have no ultimate truth, reality, or power, the less we become embroiled and enmeshed in our "stuff."

## A Mantra of Awakening

When we are fully awake, this mantra will have embedded itself within our consciousness.

It will have become our new operating system.

We will know, beyond all doubt and fear, that only the Divine is real, true, and powerful.

And that everything else has no ultimate reality at all.

Sudden, profound awakenings often include the realization that nothing outside of the divine Self has any truth, reality, or power.

Experiencing such an awakening would make reading the rest of this book unnecessary.

We do not need to learn anything about our overcoats when we know in every moment that they are not real or true, and have no power over us.

Until we reach that exalted state, it can be helpful to learn to recognize the various layers of our overcoats.

Seeing our overcoats for what they are begins the process of shedding them.

As we get to know our overcoats, the glue of unconsciousness that has bound them to us begins to dissolve.

Bringing consciousness to our overcoats reveals that none of them has anything to do with the eternal, divine Self.

The faster we remind ourselves that not one overcoat has any truth, reality, or power, the faster they fall away.

And the more overcoats that peel off, the lighter and freer we feel.

This section of the book has focused on the inner alignments that expedite awakening.

These are the consciousness keys that unlock the doors to your true Self.

As you become familiar with them, your journey of awakening automatically picks up momentum.

For now you are not resisting or delaying the process of awakening.

You are fully on board for the ride of your life!

# PART THREE

✣ ✣ ✣

# The Anatomy
# of Our Overcoats

✣ ✣ ✣

# 16

# The Veils that Obscure the True Self

*Our thoughts, our words, and our deeds*
*are the threads of the net*
*which we throw around ourselves.*

*Swami Vivekananda*

**Recognizing who and what we are not** and **realizing who we really are** comprise the two primary facets of awakening.

They are complementary and mutually reinforcing.

As we see through the disguises of our overcoats, we release our attachment to them.

We also let go of our identification with them.

Once we know they are not who we are, our overcoats have no reason to go on burdening us.

As overcoats fall away, we live more fully as the luminous Self we truly are.

And when we live as our true Self, our inner radiance naturally and inevitably burns away more of our overcoats.

In reality, these two aspects of awakening often occur simultaneously.

But for now, we'll separate them and deal with them in sequence so each receives our full attention and awareness.

First, we will focus on taking off overcoats.

Then, we will be ready to directly experience our divinity.

That is the whole point — the sacred purpose — of learning how to help our overcoats fall away.

Getting to know our overcoats will help us to recognize them so we can let them go.

They are the veils of illusion that conceal the light of our souls.

If we want more of our divine radiance to shine out into the world, we will need to master some ways to help our overcoats fall away.

That entails learning about the various layers of what we are wearing, and how they got there.

## How Did These Overcoats Pile Up?

As many of us are realizing, we are far more than the figure we see in the mirror.

Our true nature spans many dimensions and arenas of Creation.

As multidimensional souls, each of us came to Earth to explore the possibilities for experience this domain of existence offers.

In the process, most of us became so entranced with the incredibly stimulating sensory realm of 3-D that we quickly lost touch with our larger, non-physical nature.

We forgot our magnificent vastness and bought into the illusion that we were small, earthbound, human beings.

Each of us seemed to be a separate entity, alone and isolated.

Seeing one another in our bodily disguises made it all too easy to forget that we are actually always interconnected, united forever within the One Great Being.

As we lost touch with the One that is our Source, we found ourselves less able to access the love, wisdom, power, and other divine aspects of our true Self.

Our amnesia veiled from our awareness the untold riches within us.

They never went away -- it only seemed so from our limited human perspective.

Acting out of this shrunken, mistaken sense of self, we created a lot of distortion and suffering.

When traumatic events happened, we believed the pain and suffering we experienced told the truth about us.

At times, what occurred was so overwhelming, we didn't want to feel what was going on.

Our bodies, the precious temples of our souls, shut down and went numb.

We couldn't feel all of the emotions that were present.

There were too many, and they seemed too intense and scary to face.

So they went underground, waiting for a time when they could be fully felt and released.

They wrapped themselves around us as overcoats, hiding the divine light that forever shines within us.

As thoughts and judgments crowded our brains, we didn't know what to do with them all.

Each time we believed these limiting ideas were true, the clear knowing of Infinite Intelligence was obscured, leaving us feeling lost and confused.

Overcoats contain all of the things we *thought* were true about us, but are not.

The unconscious decisions we made about who we were and how life could be piled up and grew heavier.

Our overcoats squished and smothered the life force within us, limiting the range of possibilities we could experience and envision.

Gradually, one overcoat after another accumulated until all we could see about ourselves was our overcoats.

The light of our true Self was now hidden from our awareness.

We decided, *I am these overcoats.*

This left us feeling alone and separate from ourselves, other beings, and our divine Source.

## Past and Future Overcoats

Wearing so many overcoats takes us out of the present moment, the only moment we have.

Overcoats are about the past and future.

They contain all of the disappointment, regret, embarrassment, and shame -- and every other emotion— we carry about our past actions.

Even pride in our accomplishments, which can seem like a positive emotion, may become an overlay that distracts us from being here now.

When we're not busy obsessing about what went on in the past, we are likely to be worried and fearful about what might happen in the future.

Overcoats related to future concerns keep us busy trying to control our lives.

We plan and schedule and use the mind to try to influence what unfolds.

We adopt a host of other strategic behaviors that have nothing to do with being in the present moment.

Even happy anticipation of an upcoming event can take us out of the richness of this moment.

The Self lives in the Here and Now, while overcoats exist in the There and Then.


## The Burden of Our Overcoats

When we become aware of all the overcoats we are wearing, it can feel overwhelming.

At first, our overcoats can seem so heavy and tangled together that it seems we will never be free of them.

Will we ever shed enough layers to allow our divine light to shine out into the world?

Despair and hopelessness about the overcoats can pile on more layers of overcoats.

How will we ever come out from under them all?

Our fear and frustration may lead us into reacting against our overcoats.

We may employ severe spiritual disciplines and techniques, hoping to nuke them into oblivion.

Once we realize our overcoats are not who we really are, we may feel justified in rejecting them and using harsh methods in our struggle to free ourselves from them.

Or, we might try a seemingly gentler approach that is just as lacking in empathy for and acceptance of the overcoats.

We may try to ascend above and beyond our overcoats into the spiritual realms.

We might experiment with various ways of altering our consciousness, to avoid dealing with our overcoats.

*None of that stuff is ultimately real*, we may tell ourselves and others.

*Why engage with it at all?*

The escapism of such spiritual bypassing can become a way of life.

After soaring in the rarefied realms, our consciousness returns to Earth only to discover that our overcoats are just as thick and burdensome as ever.

When everything we've tried fails to free us from our overcoats, we may attempt to cover them with a shiny new exterior that, just like all the other overcoats, has nothing to do with who we really are.

These strategies add more overcoats to the heavy layers we are already wearing.

We can become so tired of wearing our overcoats, and so ashamed that they exist at all, that we will do anything to get them gone.

The world responds to our collective guilt and shame, our despair and hopelessness, with endless offers of the next magic bullet guaranteed to free us forever from our burdens.

Some of us have devoted decades to pursuing anything that seems to promise release from the weight of our overcoats.

But the truth is that overcoats only come off when they are ready.

The simple act of bringing consciousness to them begins the process of their dissolution.

As quantum physics demonstrates, the mere presence of an observer changes the outcome of an experiment.

And witnessing the presence of overcoats, without trying to do anything about them, begins the process of their dissolution.

Although they appear heavy and substantial, we start to realize there is nothing real or lasting about them.

When the light of consciousness shines upon them, they are revealed for what they are -- temporary illusions that have nothing to do with the eternal truth of our beingness.

So there is no need to try to get rid of our overcoats, or to banish them to the Hall of Shame where we hope no one else ever sees them.

No need to hide them or pretend they don't exist.

We don't have to "work on" them or try to "transform" them.

When enough awareness has been brought to our overcoats, when we have met them with love and compassion and absolute acceptance, they simply fall away, revealing the magnificence of who we really are.

## The Planetary Field of Possibility

There is another factor that comes to our aid as we face and embrace our overcoats.

We live in an extraordinary time.

The field of expanded energy~consciousness surrounding the planet is stronger and brighter than ever before.

That means it is easier than ever to bring awareness to whatever has accumulated within us, hiding the light that we are.

And when we become aware of what is present, it can dissolve and drop away more quickly than ever before.

That is why it is now possible to move through issues and challenges that might have taken years or even decades to surmount in the past.

Overcoats it once might have taken many lifetimes to release can now come off much more rapidly.

And as any one of us releases overcoats, it becomes that much easier for all of us to let our overcoats go.

When one among us remembers s/he is a divine Self, the spark of the One in us all shines a little more brightly.

For we are all part of a great, unified Beingness, and what happens within any one of us instantly affects all others.

## The True Self is Bombproof

Finally, it helps to remember that no matter how heavy and thick our overcoats may seem, they can never obliterate who we truly are.

Nothing that happens here on Earth can ever change, damage, distort, or destroy the Self.

Not even the most trauma-filled life can ever snuff out the light that radiates from within our heart of hearts.

No experience — no overcoat — has that kind of power.

Beneath all the overcoats, who we really are is always still there: the eternal, unchanging divinity of the Self.

Our essential Self may be underground, buried beneath layers of overcoats, but it never goes away.

The true Self forever lives within, waiting for our awareness to return to it.

Waiting for us to remember that we ARE it.

The following chapters present the primary layers of our overcoats.

Bringing awareness to these layers allows them to peel back, revealing what lies beneath them all -- the true, divine Self.

Layer by layer, we find our way Home.

# 17

# Bodily Sensations

*Although the world is full of suffering,*
*it is also full of overcoming it.*

*Helen Keller*

As we turn our awareness toward our inner world, sensations in the physical body are often what we notice first.

Try this for a moment.

Invite your eyes to close, and see what you become aware of within yourself.

The first thing your awareness may pick up are the sensations that accompany your breathing.

You might also discover other bodily sensations.

A dull ache in a shoulder, a sharp pain in the low back, a tight clenching in the throat, a congested blob in the belly — a wide range of bodily sensations may present themselves.

Our bodies tend to store residues from past experiences.

A few hours of gardening yesterday might have left some aching muscles that will feel better by tomorrow.

The energetic remnants from a traumatic event decades ago may have settled more deeply into the body's tissues, possibly creating a chronic condition of dis-ease.

Not all body-sensations become overcoats.

Those that are able to be felt can move through easily.

During morning yoga, we stretch and breathe into an area of tightness, and before long the contraction releases and we feel the body opening and lengthening.

Practices such as ta'i chi and qi gong encourage body-awareness, which helps to keep our energetic channels open.

When we attend to the body's messages, we are choosing to deal with discomfort and pain rather than ignoring or denying it.

When bodily knots and contractions are not given this kind of attention and build up over time, chronic areas of tightness and dis-ease can develop.

These, along with any thoughts and feelings that go with them, become woven into our overcoats.

By the time we've been here a while, most of us are wearing at least a few overcoats of physical discomfort.

Each one of them is a place that, to at least some degree, has shut down or closed off to the neverending flow of life energy.

Bodily aches and pains may appear to have become permanent fixtures, but bringing awareness and the breath into them can help them to open back up.

Sometimes, the basic practice of breathing into and feeling body-sensations can lead to the release of long-held tension.

The body feels newly born, fresh and clear of stored discord.

Such big results from such a simple practice can seem miraculous.

Later in this book, guided, inner Experiences will lead you through this simple practice.

# 18

# Emotions

*We know too much*
*and feel too little.*

*Bertrand Russell*

Right behind or within physical sensations, emotions such as sadness and frustration are waiting to be felt.

These comprise the next layer we encounter when we become aware of what is happening in our inner world.

Many of us have spent a lifetime trying our best to *not* feel our feelings.

We stop ourselves from crying, hold in our anger, and take out our frustration on inanimate objects.

"Get a grip on yourself," we tell the face in the mirror.

We become embarrassed and ashamed if, despite our best intentions, others glimpse what is really going on inside us.

All of these unallowed, unfelt feelings pile up to create some very thick overcoats.

And more overcoats accumulate when we judge our feelings and shut off to them.

Even emotions we consider "positive" can end up in our overcoats when we say NO to them.

We may feel love, but for one reason or another we do not let ourselves fully experience it, much less express it.

Or perhaps we feel excited about something, but in our desire to be seen as a sophisticated, understated person, we muffle our energy instead of letting it express with the exuberance we feel.

Any emotion we judge as inappropriate ends up layering into our overcoats.

In not letting it be what it is, we stop the free flow of our life energy.

When we are awake, living as the Self, we experience this moment of life, and then the next, and the next.

Whatever is present within us is allowed to be exactly as it is.

But when something happens that we say NO to, our energy gets backed up.

We cannot fully be with what is going on right now, because we haven't finished being with what happened in the past.

This is how overcoats pile up.

Whatever we couldn't fully be with goes underground.

It may seem as if we have completed it, but it is still there, waiting for us to return to it and finish feeling what we could not feel at the time.

We may also cling to times that felt good.

We wish we could stay in those moments forever.

When we habitually pull out fond memories from the past and relive them, we are caught in the overcoats of the past.

Whether we cling to or resist our feelings, overcoats accumulate.

## Venting Feelings

We can do three things with our feelings.

One option is to vent them — express them outwardly, usually toward someone or something else.

Often, when we do this, we blame the other person for what we are feeling.

"He made me so mad!"

"She hurt my feelings."

Since we believe our feelings are "their fault," we then feel justified in blasting them with the full force of our emotional reaction.

"I told him where to go!"

"I said I never really liked her anyway."

When we vent, it can seem as though we are expressing our feelings.

But outwardly reacting means we are not in touch with what is going on inside of ourselves.

Our buttons have been pushed, but we do not realize what we are truly feeling.

Instead, our knee-jerk reaction usually only makes the situation worse.

Venting is a sign that we have put someone else in the driver's seat of our life.

We believe that person has "made us mad" or "hurt us."

We remain centered in our true Self when we recognize that others' actions are about *them* — they have nothing to do with us.

And our reactions have nothing to do with them.

They are going on *within us*.

When we are able to be with ourselves and experience what is truly going on within, we do not vent our feelings.

We simply feel them.

We may also become aware of the overcoats the challenging interaction has brought to the surface of our awareness.

As we see them for what they are, they automatically begin to dissolve and fall away.

## Repressing Feelings

As we have seen, **venting** is one way we can deal with uncomfortable feelings.

The second thing we can do with our feelings is **repress them**.

At all costs, we keep them hidden.

We shove our feelings down and pretend we don't feel anything at all.

Then we wonder why we feel so dead and lifeless inside.

The famous "stiff upper lip" of the British is all about not revealing what we're feeling -- even to ourselves.

When repression becomes a way of life, we feel proud of our ability to not let on that anything bothers us.

We often adopt this strategy when others have used our feelings in an attempt to induce guilt or shame.

Powerful figures in our lives may have responded to feelings we've expressed in ways that make us sorry we ever revealed anything at all.

Here is what repression sounds like:

"I know I have a lot of fears, but I don't go there."

"It's a lot to deal with, but I try not to let it get to me."

"Stuff happens. You just have to get up and keep going."

We may even deny our feelings when there is clear, overt evidence that they are going on.

Haven't we all witnessed someone saying, "I'm not angry!" in a vehement tone while physically shaking or showing other signs of intense emotion?

But when we repress our feelings, they don't go away.

They continue to fester deep inside.

We may feel clogged, sodden with unshed tears or boiling with pent-up anger.

Our bottled-up feelings may turn into bodily symptoms, another attempt at getting our attention.

Or those around us may reflect what we are not willing to face in ourselves.

In exaggerated ways, others may express the feelings we shove down.

A woman who has deemed her anger unacceptable may wonder, "Why is everybody so angry all the time?"

A man who prides himself on his rationality might comment, "She's so emotional -- I wish she'd get a grip."

A freeway driver whose inner rule book insists on being "nice" at all times may exclaim, "Do you believe he just cut me off and then flipped me the bird?"

Neither venting nor repressing offers us the ease of emotional expression that contributes to a healthy, happy life.

Generalizations can be risky, but in general:

We vent feelings when we believe "**you** *should be different.*"

We repress feelings when we believe "*I should be different.*"

Either way, we are not simply being with the emotion that is present within us.

Either way, overcoats are accumulating.

## A Third Way: Being with Feelings

If venting and repressing are not the best ways to deal with our feelings, what is?

There is a third way, one that doesn't involve blasting our feelings out into the atmosphere like a nuclear explosion, or its opposite, bottling them up inside until we fear a volcanic eruption might ensue if we ever go near them.

When we do not vent or repress our feelings, we take responsibility for what we are experiencing.

We do not make it "their fault" or "my fault."

What we are feeling is really no one's fault.

It simply is what it is.

Since most of us have rarely seen anyone model this, it is understandable that we may not know anything other than venting and repressing is possible.

Our planet is inundated by the suffering of venting and repressing.

Individually and collectively, neither venting nor repressing offers us a road to emotional freedom.

So, how do we find our way onto that road?

The way is quite simple.

Whenever a feeling arises, we meet it with our presence and awareness.

We do not reject it and shove it down.

Neither do we vent it and unleash a nuclear chain-reaction of emotion.

We simply feel the feeling.

We breathe into the sensations that are present and let them be what they are, experiencing them fully.

We do this without any attempt to rationalize or explain why the feeling is there, what caused it, or how to get rid of it.

The mind may want to get busy with all of this, and we may need to remind ourselves that is optional, and not advised.

All we need to do is return to breathing and feeling whatever is present.

An attitude of open-ended inquiry can be helpful:

*What is this feeling attempting to communicate?*

*What does it want me to know about itself?*

*What can I learn about myself through this experience?*

We don't need to get busy solving the problem our feeling seems to present.

We don't need to know what to do next, or to hatch a plan.

All we need to do is feel what we're feeling.

Often, spiritual seekers judge their feelings as being a hindrance or a distraction on the path.

*"If only I could get past these painful feelings, I could really get somewhere spiritually."*

*"If I don't get a handle on this anger, I'll never awaken."*

*"I'm so scared of so many things. What a joke to think I could go beyond all of that."*

But our feelings are not IN the way, they ARE the way.

A sacred path opens out before us when we are willing to simply be with whatever is arising and feel it fully.

If we follow this path all the way, we end up at the doorway to the true Self.

We don't need to be afraid of our emotional "stuff," for whatever is arising offers us the next step on our journey Home.

## Feelings and Overcoats

Every soul in the human experience has a full range of emotions it is here to taste, to feel, and to savor while it is here on Earth.

For instance, when someone we love makes the Great Transition and is no longer here among us, we miss them and feel sad.

That grief is normal.

It is part of the rich banquet of life a soul comes here to experience.

A feeling only becomes an overcoat when we judge or separate from our experience -- when we make it wrong.

Overcoats pile on when the mind convinces us thoughts like these are true:

*"It's been six months. I shouldn't still be crying every day."*

Or: *"Friends are telling me I should be getting on with my life. Maybe they're right."*

When we believe the mind's ideas about what we ought to be doing and feeling, we can lose touch with what is really going on within ourselves.

Then, we might adopt mental strategies to manage our experience, to manipulate it into being something else that is more acceptable to some part of us.

When that happens, we are no longer in the realm of pure experience.

We are not letting what is present be what it is.

We're trying to make it into something the mind says is OK.

Conversely, when we are able to let ourselves feel what is present, no overcoats accumulate.

When a feeling arises and we let it be, it can be felt and released right away.

Nothing sticks; nothing is accumulated.

This capacity is alive and well in young children.

When they are upset, they shout, scream, and cry.

In short, they get it all out.

Within minutes, they are playing and laughing again as if nothing had happened.

No residue of their previous upset remains.

We are never too old to rediscover this ability.

All it takes is saying YES instead of NO to whatever arises.

We don't need to throw a tantrum or break things; that would be venting.

The key is to feel what we're feeling and then let it pass through.

This may require more conscious attention than it does in a small child, because most of us have shut down our feeling capacities to at least some extent.

If traumatic events occurred in our past, as they have for most of us, we probably weren't able to fully feel everything that was going on at the time.

It was too big, or too scary, or someone gave us the message that our feelings were not welcome.

Those unfelt feelings went underground and became part of our overcoats.

The more unfelt feeling, the thicker the layers of "unfinished business" veiling our inner radiance.

We compound the emotional layers of our overcoats by judging our feelings and separating from them.

Then, not only the unfelt feelings pile up, but also all the ideas we have about them.

All the shoulds and shouldn'ts:

*"I should be over this by now."*

*"What happened was not such a big deal -- why am I still so upset about it?"*

*"I shouldn't be feeling this."*

*"I don't want to be someone who cries all the time."*

*"I hate myself -- I'm such an emotional mess."*

It's hard enough to be walking around beneath layers of overcoats full of leftover feelings from the past.

We don't need to make it even harder by condemning ourselves for it.

The feelings will not be resolved any more easily or quickly through beating ourselves up over them.

In fact, with more overcoats of suffering wrapped around the feelings and memories, they can become harder to access.

Harder, but not impossible.

When it's time, the feelings will arise so that we can be with them instead of turning away from them.

In the meantime, we can decide to love ourselves, as is.

Not once we get past all of our troubling emotions, or when we "have a handle on them," whatever that means.

But right now, messy emotions and all.

We can be kind instead of cruel towards ourselves, no matter what we have going on or what we've been through.

That can only help the overcoats of judgment and self-blame to fall away.

And when we release those overcoats, all the others are easier to face, embrace, and let go.

## The Gift of Emotions

Feeling is an integral part of this earthly life, and we humans are capable of experiencing the entire gamut of emotions, from ecstasy and awe to listlessness and boredom.

As long as we souls inhabit human bodies, we will experience emotions.

The irresistible lure of emotions played a big part in why we each chose to come to Earth, for feelings are a central feature of embodied experience.

As nothing else can, the enormous range of feelings we humans are capable of experiencing adds spice and savor to every moment of our lives.

Imagine cooking a meal without adding in the tastes of sweet, salty, bitter, sour, and umami.

The food would be bland, boring, and unappetizing.

Human life would be similarly dull and lifeless without the zing and zest of emotions.

Whether we feel delighted or disappointed, serene or surprised, affectionate or amazed, feelings let us know we are alive.

They are expressions of our divine essence as it interacts with the world and the beings within it.

Feeling what we are feeling is being responsive to our soul, as it attempts to make us aware of deeper levels of our life experience.

Our feelings are not a problem, then, but an asset, because they tune us in to what is really going on in us and in our lives.

Feelings can remind us of places within us that are in need of our caring and compassion.

They may also function as an alarm system, alerting us to a situation that needs prompt attention.

For instance, a feeling of unease and discomfort around someone might be letting us know that it is not in our best interest to spend time with that person.

When we attend to the feeling, when we accept it as Life's way of getting our attention, we act accordingly and avoid further discomfort — or even tragedy.

When we ignore the feeling, it layers into an overcoat, where it is stored until the time we are ready and willing to be with it and acknowledge its message.

By then, more overcoats may have piled up from the traumas the original feeling was attempting to prevent us from having to experience.

Feelings also arise in response to bigger, less personal issues.

Who among us hasn't felt sadness, grief, and overwhelm when faced with the latest tragedy on the world stage?

When we do not allow time and space to feel these feelings, they pile on as overcoats.

But if we can feel the feelings, they pass through us, rather than accumulating within us.

As we feel our emotions about a troubling situation, we may find ourselves prompted to take effective action.

We might communicate through social media, share revelatory articles and videos, or take a public stand on an issue.

We may feel an inner impulse to donate money to a cause or relief effort.

When outer action arises from the inner process of becoming aware of and feeling our emotions, that action is rooted in the power of presence.

Many people use the latest distressing news as a prompting to pray.

We do not even need to know what to pray for.

We can simply add our energy to that of the Divine, asking that the highest and best outcome for all involved may unfold.

Whenever we remember to turn our outrage and grief and helplessness into prayer, the power of our emotions is channeled toward a positive outcome.

## Awakened Beings and Emotions

When we resist and repress our feelings, we dam them up.

And when we vent our emotions rather than truly feel them, they not only create more discord and chaos in the world, they also grow stronger and more stubbornly embedded within us.

Either way, the feelings are not able to pass through.

They accumulate as overcoats, hiding the divine light at our core.

Fortunately, there is another way to be with emotions.

When we give them space to be what they are, and witness and feel them as they arise, emotions are like clouds -- here one moment and gone the next.

Lying on the ground and watching clouds on a summer's day, we enjoy the beautiful shapes and patterns, free of any need or desire to try to capture and hold on to them.

We can bring that same spaciousness to our emotions.

Then, as each feeling is felt, it easily and naturally moves through to make way for the next experience Life brings.

Awakened beings are neither for nor against emotion.

That doesn't mean they sit around in some sort of glazed, emotionally-flattened state, feeling nothing at all.

On the contrary, many awakened beings experience a degree of liveliness and spontaneity most humans never approach.

When a feeling rises up, it has all the space it needs to fully be what it is.

Like a wave in the ocean, the feeling arises, crests, and then continues through, leaving no residue as it dissipates.

Strong, intense feelings of all kinds can move through those who are awake.

They may mourn the suffering of the world, or angrily rant about injustice.

The great awakened one called Ramana Maharshi said, "The realized person weeps with the weeping, laughs with the laughing, plays with the playful, [and] sings with those who sing, keeping time to the song."

Emotion in the awakened is like a summer storm -- quick to arise and just as quick to dissipate.

These beings have all the same feelings we do, but they do not identify with them or believe there is anything ultimately real or true about them.

The awakened are *in the experience of* their feelings, rather than believing they *are* their emotions, as most humans do.

As we awaken to who we really are, we find ourselves resisting our feelings less, and making space for them more easily and often.

We no longer think of our feelings as *who we are*; our identity with our habitual emotional patterns dissolves.

As we become increasingly energetically transparent, instead of clotted with feelings, our overcoats thin and fall away.

This, in turn, leaves little or no place for feelings to stick.

The feelings of awakened beings are clean and pure, not muddled with conflicting emotions, thoughts, and judgments.

Such beings feel the joy or pain of emotion, without becoming mired in the suffering of judging it or believing that something else should be going on.

Like clouds in a clear blue sky, their emotions rise up, are fully experienced, and pass through.

Until we fully reside in that sublime state, we can continue to bring as much awareness as possible to the emotional challenges we encounter along the way.

They are the catalysts that, when we can meet them with acceptance and presence, help us to shed our overcoats and rest more deeply in who we truly are.

And if our feelings ever seem too intense and frightening to handle, a wide variety of professionals can help us through them so that the radiant, luminous Self can fully blossom.

# 19

# Fear

*What must I pass through to find that place of safety?*
*I must pass through the wound because the wound is the gate.*
*How do I find the wound?*
*I find all the places that cause me pain,*
*all the places where I've believed the pain was being caused by some-*
*thing out there.*

Stephen Schwartz
*The Compassionate Presence*

Our culture teaches us to do anything but feel our fear.

We are told to ignore it, to deny it, to act like it doesn't exist.

Or, we get the message to power through it, to keep on going even if we feel terrified.

Admitting we feel fear is seen as unmanly, and these days it is also viewed as unwomanly.

No wonder so few of us go anywhere near our fear!

But acting as though we are fearless just adds more overcoats to those we are already wearing.

They are full of the fears that are already present and not being felt.

There must be another way.

How can we face our fear without giving in to it?

How might we feel our fears without letting them stop us?

As we awaken, how does our relationship to fear change?

## Fear of Feelings

Fear is a special category of feeling.

And fear, more than any other feeling, affects our ability to feel what is going on within us.

Our fear of our feelings can keep us from even going near them.

Many of us have heard ourselves say something like this:

"I'm afraid if I start to cry, I might never stop."

"If I ever really let myself feel how angry I am, I'm scared I might do some damage."

"I'm worried people will think I'm crazy if I ever reveal how intense my feelings are."

We might also notice deep, unconscious beliefs about our feelings.

They might sound like this:

*My feelings are way more powerful than I know what to do with. They're bigger than I am.*

*If I open the door to my feelings, I'll be overwhelmed, swept away in the deluge.*

*So many feelings have built up inside that I'll be nonfunctional if I ever start to let them out. My life will fall apart.*

*If I ever show others all of my feelings, they will decide I'm crazy -- sick -- and reject me.*

If these beliefs were true, it certainly wouldn't make sense to go anywhere near our feelings.

But are they?

Do we really know for sure what will happen if we walk up to the edge of that knot of fear in our belly, sit down beside it and befriend it?

Is it certain that we will get swept into a black hole of emotion from which we will never emerge?

It is possible to question our fears, rather than automatically believing them.

This puts us back in the center of our lives, instead of at the edge, grasping for something to hang on to.

Our fear of our feelings can cause us to adopt coping strategies.

Some of us vehemently deny that we even *have* any troubling feelings.

Others live in their heads, explaining away their feelings without ever feeling them.

There are those who make their lives all about practicalities, leaving no room for feelings.

These people often say, "I'm too busy to have any feelings."

Another version of this is saying, whenever a challenge arises, "Just deal with it."

Our fear of our feelings can keep us from feeling anything at all.

As we become aware that the fear of our emotions is keeping us from feeling, we realize how dry and lifeless our existence has become.

When we fear our feelings yet sense it would be helpful to move toward them, we can begin by simply acknowledging that fear is present.

We learn to recognize the telltale signs of fear as it manifests in us.

Bodily symptoms such as a knotted-up belly, a tight throat, a clenched jaw.

Mind-stuff: *What's the point in stirring up that hornets' nest? Leave it alone.*

Emotional reactions: Anger, when someone suggests it might be helpful to investigate our feelings around an issue. Prickliness. Guardedness. Defensiveness.

And the classic strategies of our overcoats to get us to look anywhere but at them:

Distraction.

Avoidance.

Denial.

Glossing over.

Belittling the importance of what we are feeling.

Recognizing these signs that fear is present is a first step in facing and eventually embracing our fears.


## Fear of Our Fears

If we fear our feelings, we probably **really** fear our fears.

Many of us find that our fear of our fear keeps us from even admitting we have any fears.

"Me, afraid? No way."

This can result in a life that resembles a series of movie stunts.

It's all action and adventure, with little or no interior awareness.

These people wear overcoats of avoidance, denial, and rejection of feeling.

They are not free to *have* feelings -- emotions must be controlled, managed, limited, curtailed.

If the opposite reaction takes hold, people find their lives circumscribed by all the fears they don't know they have.

They give themselves a million reasons why it doesn't make sense to take risks, when all the while their unconscious fears load them up with overcoats.

In either case, whether we are more like a daredevil or a shrinking violet, fear is at the root of our outer behavior.

Fear we don't even know we have.

Our unconscious fears cause us to do, or not do, all kinds of things.

We may believe our conscious minds are at the helm of our lives, when, in reality, these deep-seated fears we do not even know are there lead us to "decide" and "choose" to live in limited ways.

A fundamental issue, then, is whether we can even admit that fears are present within us.

We may need some evidence to accept that.

If we are not willing and able to be with whatever is arising in the current moment -- if we shut down our awareness with our addiction of choice many times during each day -- it is probably because unconscious fears prevent us from going near what is happening.

And since fear lies at the bottom of many other feelings, our fear of our fear may prevent us from feeling the other emotions that are present.

It's as if something in us knows that if we begin to feel what is there, the trail may well take us down, down, down into the subterranean realm where fear lives.

And then what?

The black hole syndrome.

We feel sure that we will be sucked down, never to reappear again.

We fear being overwhelmed by the fears lurking there.

We fear we are inadequate to confront them -- they seem bigger and stronger than we are.

We might believe we need to know how to deal with the fears.

Maybe we think we should know how to make them go away.

And since we don't have a clue about how to do that, it may seem to make more sense to just not go there.

But this is not the way we get free.

So, the challenge is: Can we admit that fears are present within us?

Once we confess that, it is possible to go toward the fears and see what they reveal about themselves.

It helps to remember that every fear is based on a belief (more about this in the next chapter).

We can often hear the belief within the fear itself.

"I'm afraid if I ever start to look at my fears, they will take over my life."

Do you hear the belief in that fear-statement?

The degree to which a fear runs our life exactly correlates with how strongly we agree that the underlying belief is true.

And the amount of unfelt fear within us dictates how many of our other emotions we are willing to face and go into.

As we begin to admit that fear lies within us, we find ourselves more able to be with the other emotions that are also present.

The universal antidote for fear is love.

When we can find love and compassion for ourselves and what we are experiencing, we are more able to face and embrace whatever is there.

Cultivating self-empathy while developing the consciousness skills presented in this book enables us to turn toward our feelings instead of away from them.

We stop relegating them to the back alley of our psyche, and invite them in.

Making a place at the table for our emotions, we pour them a cup of tea.

As we get to know some of our milder, less-threatening feelings, we feel emboldened to keep going toward the deeper, stronger ones.

We discover that our fear of our feelings was much scarier than the feelings themselves.

Overcoats of repression peel away, and a lighter, brighter sense of self and life emerges from beneath them.

# 20

# The Contents of the Mind

*Thoughts pass in my mind*
*like flocks of ducks in the sky.*
*I hear the voice of their wings.*

Rabindranath Tagore
*Moon, For What Do You Wait?*

You may notice that as you bring awareness to your feelings and fears, thoughts are also present.

There is a good reason for that.

Feelings arise from thoughts -- ideas and concepts we believe to be true.

These beliefs "justify" our feelings.

They "give us a reason" to feel what we are feeling.

In the same way, each fear that is present within us is based on a belief.

We avoid looking at our fears because we subconsciously believe the underlying ideas they are based on are true.

## The Mind Is Not a Neutral Observer

The mind does its best to convince us that it is objective and rational.

As a result, many of us never question the thoughts the mind insists are true.

This leads to a great deal of suffering.

We believe what the mind says, since it does such a good job of appearing to be logical.

But the mind is not an impartial observer of life.

The mind prefers to believe its *interpretations* of events, rather than simply observing those events.

Any number of interpretations can result from the same action.

For instance, Jeremy sees a $200 balance in his checkbook and feels fear.

"The rent is due in two days. What will the landlord do if I can't pay it? I'm afraid I'll be out on the street."

Seeing his low checkbook balance not only brings up present fears, it also unconsciously reminds this young man of other times when he felt incapable of managing his life.

Deeper fears may lurk within: "What if I never get my life together? Could there be something wrong with me?"

These fears imply beliefs: *I don't know how to get my life together. There is something wrong with me.*

We react as we do to life's events based on not only what seems to be going on at the surface level, but also these deep-seated beliefs about ourselves and life -- beliefs we are largely ignorant are there.

For example, we tend to think it "makes sense" to react with anger when we decide we have been slighted.

We are not aware that it was our *interpretation* of events, not the events themselves, that led to that decision, and to the feelings of anger.

In the same way, most of us would say it is "reasonable" to react with fear when our bankbook indicates we have $200 to our name.

Most humans believe these knee-jerk feeling-responses (to thoughts we do not know are even there) are inevitable and unavoidable.

But that isn't true.

Enlightened beings have dissociated thoughts from feeling-reactions, and we can, too.

A key to detaching thoughts from feelings is to question the thoughts.

Consciousness teacher Byron Katie likes to say, "Our thoughts aren't the problem. We only get into trouble when we believe them."

The first step is to recognize the thoughts that are there in the mind.

The second step is to see the thoughts for what they are -- *ideas* about reality, not the truth.

Believing them is optional.

The fact that buying into the thoughts is optional puts a lot of space around them -- space in which they can simply be as they are.

We do not have to be for or against the thoughts.

We don't even need to be for or against the fact that the mind is full of thoughts.

Legions of people have attempted to meditate and given up, saying, "I couldn't get my thoughts to stop."

They had somehow gotten the message that this is the goal of meditation.

But the nature of mind is to generate thoughts.

That is what mind does.

Trying to get the mind to stop generating thoughts is as pointless as telling a happy dog not to wag its tail.

When people fail to stop their thoughts during meditation, many conclude that meditating is a waste of time.

But the real waste of time turns out to be trying to stop the mind!

So does that mean we should just sit back and let the mind go wild?

Should we live our lives based on what the mind says is true?

Not if we want to experience any kind of peace in this life.

We won't ever stop the mind from generating thoughts.

What we **can** do, though, is step back from the thoughts and *witness* them.

We can bring the power of awareness to the ideas and concepts the mind endlessly spins and become conscious of what the thoughts are saying.

And what the thoughts *behind* the thoughts are saying.

We can see them all for what they are -- beliefs, ideas, and concepts about reality.

They are not reality itself!

The simple act of recognizing this causes the inner cacophony of thoughts to quiet over time.

As we see the thoughts have no ultimate truth or power, we stop giving energy to what the mind generates.

When a being grasps this truth, the gift of grace called liberation from the mind arrives.

## Thoughts and Truth

Thoughts on their own can do no damage.

They are just thoughts -- harmless and innocent until we buy into them and make them The Way It Is.

They have no power over us unless we give them that power.

The power lies in us, not in the thoughts.

The thoughts that we have deemed true pile up and compact together into a very thick overcoat indeed.

It consists of all the ideas we believe about the way we ought to be, how our lives should be unfolding, and every other aspect of our existence.

Every belief we have said YES to, every concept we have accepted as true, becomes a part of this overcoat of suffering.

For some of us, this heavy garment has become so thick and unwieldy we can barely move.

We feel paralyzed by indecision.

This idea about how to be and live goes against that one.

What are we to do?

A first step is to recognize a fundamental difference.

There is the swarm of ideas around which we have molded our reality, and then there is the truth of our innermost being.

When the truth of our essential Self is revealed, and we go with it, we feel a sense of internal coherence.

Everything in us lines up in a pattern of wholeness and harmony, like metal filings gathering around a magnet.

In contrast, when we live according to what the mind is saying, we never quite feel settled in ourselves.

We constantly second-guess our decisions.

We struggle to stay afloat in a swamp of chaotic thoughts.

Mind begets mind.

In most human beings, unquestioned thoughts continuously spawn more of the same.

No wonder we so often feel as if we are going around in circles!

So how can we help the thick overcoat of mind peel away?

We can bring the light of consciousness into it and see the thoughts for what they are -- ideas, not reality.

When we believe the thoughts, we suffer.

Releasing ourselves from suffering, then, depends on our ability to see the thoughts for what they are and to give them no authority over us or our lives.

The simple act of observing thoughts rather than automatically believing them has the power to change our existence.

We don't need to try to change the thoughts.

There's no point in focusing on improving or upleveling them.

That would only breed more thoughts!

All we need to do is witness them, and give them no power.

We can decide to be kind to ourselves and others rather than believing the endless mental litany of criticism and judgment.

We can choose to tell ourselves, "These are only thoughts -- they are not true unless I say so!"

And why would we want to say YES to thoughts that have nothing to do with the truth of our soul?

## Fear and Belief

Just as feelings are based in thoughts, each of our fears is also rooted in at least one thought — and often, many.

One fear may reflect a host of ideas about life, not just a single belief.

We feel fear based on what we believe is true.

If we believe it is a cold, heartless world, our fears stem from that belief.

When we decide the thoughts that insist we are not lovable are true, we fear getting close to others and being rejected.

If we agree with the mind's ideas that earning a living is hard and money is scarce, our fears likely center on sustenance issues.

These fears and beliefs run our lives -- until we examine them and see them for what they are.

Until we remember that believing them is always and forever **optional**.

And that our thoughts have no power except the power we have given them.

There is a simple way to become aware of our fears and the underlying thoughts we have subconsciously accepted as true.

The process of dismantling the confining cage of our fears and beliefs is twofold.

First, we ask to be made aware of a fear that has a big impact on our life.

It helps to write it down.

This gets it out of the subconscious and onto paper, where we can see it more clearly.

Then, we can ask to be made aware of the beliefs beneath the fear.

We then write them down below the fear statement.

An example may make the process easier to follow.

Phoebe has decided to examine some of her fears and the beliefs beneath them.

She writes, *I feel afraid that no one will ever really love me.*

Below the fear statement, Phoebe lists the beliefs that give rise to the fear:

*No one will ever really love me.*

*I will always be alone and unhappy.*

*I've had too many disappointments in life and no one will ever want to hear about them all.*

*I feel awkward around others, especially men who seem interesting to me, and this will turn them off.*

And so on.

She may fill a page or more with beliefs that "explain" her fear.

If Phoebe buys into these beliefs, her fear will seem justified.

But as we are coming to realize, believing the mind's ideas is optional and only leads to suffering.

So, after listing all the beliefs that surface, Phoebe examines each one and asks if it is true.

She finds that she cannot say for sure that no one will ever love her, or that she will always be alone and unhappy.

Through examining her mind's beliefs, Phoebe is developing the ability to *witness* her thoughts rather than give power to them.

# 21

# Judgments

*If you want peace of mind
do not find fault with others.*

*Sarada Devi*

You have probably already noticed that many of the thoughts that come and go are actually judgments.

The judgments may be of yourself, others, God, or life itself.

Humans judge everything — from cars to animals to the foods they eat.

A lot of what we call gossip is actually socially sanctioned judging.

A thought that contains an evaluation, a comparison, or the idea that someone or something should be different is a judgment.

Occasionally, humans deem something or someone to be "good" or "nice," but most judgments are negative or condemning.

And judgments vary in the severity of their impact.

One level of judgment consists of finding fault with, say, a washing machine or a restaurant meal.

We might even criticize someone's behavior:

"He acted way too quickly in that situation, before he had all the facts."

"She didn't stop nagging her daughter long enough to congratulate her on winning that prize."

Although such statements are evaluative and often inaccurate, this is a relatively minor aspect of judging.

An entirely different level of judgment is expressed in statements that harshly evaluate someone's *very beingness*.

"That's just the way he is." (Here the judgment is implied, and listeners are unlikely to conclude that it is a positive one.)

"She's a stupid idiot."

"He's a worthless jerk."

Swear words are often used to literally curse those to whom they are spoken.

No wonder many still refer to using these words as "cursing."

We say that "sticks and stones can break my bones, but names can never hurt me."

But how many people who were verbally abused as children never overcome the "curses" they received?

When our very being is regularly reviled, how are we to develop positive self-esteem?

It's one thing to object to someone's behavior.

It's quite another to lay waste to their basic, inherent goodness.

Whenever we stand in judgment of someone, we are caught in the delusion that we are entitled to condemn that person's being, not merely their behavior.

The only level of consciousness that is capable of viewing everything about a being, and is therefore able to evaluate it, belongs to the totality we call God.

And the Divine never judges!

The One recognizes we are each in the process of evolving toward full soul-embodiment and expression, and all along the way we are likely to act from the forgetting and limitations of our humanness.

We are forever held in love and forgiveness as we make our way through the confusing labyrinth of the Earth-plane toward complete awakening.

Only the human caught in forgetting judges.

As we awaken, judging drops away.

Through awakened eyes, we see that each of us is doing the very best we are capable of, and when we can do better, we will.

Awakening replaces judgment with empathy and compassion.


## Judgments Imply Comparison

Judgments imply or state outright that something or someone is "bad" or "wrong" -- or "good" and "right," when the judgment is a positive one.

Judging statements don't always include the words "should" or "ought," but they often do.

These words may also be implied.

"I'm too picky" implies the speaker ought to be less so, in her judgment.

We can also spot judgments by the comparisons they contain, whether overt or implicit.

"I'm too fat." (In comparison to whom, or to which standard?)

"That driver is going way too slow." (Notice the word "too" -- it usually means judging is going on.)

When we accept things as they are, we don't use words like "should" and "too" to describe them.

If judging thoughts are arising, and we buy into them, we are no longer fully present with What Is.

We are not feeling our feelings or being with what is really going on within.

We are on automatic pilot, accepting the mind's judgments instead of questioning them.

When we believe judging thoughts, we distance ourselves and separate from the object of the judgment.

If the judgment is against ourselves, a part of us -- the judging mind -- turns against the rest of us, or a particular aspect of our being or behavior.

If the judgment is about someone else, we are no longer united with that person within the field of Life that holds all beings in interconnected harmony.

We have separated ourselves from that being and may now see her as an adversary rather than a sister human being with the same fundamental feelings and challenges we have.

When our awareness is entrained to the human mind and unquestioningly believes its assessments, it feels good to judge others.

We buy into the illusion that we raise ourselves up with each put-down of another.

We puff ourselves up and feel invincible.

But deep down inside, those who frequently judge others are burdened by heavy overcoats of harsh, unforgiving, and unspoken judgments of themselves.

Judgment reflects a belief that we are all here on Earth to strive toward some unattainable ideal of perfection.

Judgment is also based in believing that we can be other than what we really are -- divine beings of light.

Not even the thickest layers of overcoats can in any way change who we truly are.

Holding ourselves or others to an impossible standard, we fail to see the tender, vulnerable shoots of life that are doing their best to blossom beneath the crushing overcoats of unrelenting perfectionism.

What we judge in others is nearly always what we cannot accept in ourselves.

If we see others as lazy and shiftless, we probably don't let ourselves relax very often.

If "they" appear to be spendthrifts, maybe we need to let loose and splurge once in a while.

If others' homes are not up to our standards of cleanliness and order, it could be time to experiment with letting the cleaning go for a week to find out the judgments and fears of others' reactions that brings up.

Most of us have no idea how often and how harshly we judge.

The mind convinces us we are being "objective" when what is really going on is condemnation and cruelty.

The more ruthlessly and unforgivingly we judge others, the more mercilessly we judge ourselves when no one is looking.

Since judgment is often unconscious, we may have no idea how relentlessly unforgiving we are being to those around us, or the precious life-form that we are.

## The Life-Annihilating Power of Judgment

In the previous chapter we met Phoebe, who began to examine a deep fear that no one will ever really love her.

When Phoebe investigated the thoughts behind this fear, she not only discovered the beliefs she looked into in the previous chapter.

She also came upon several judgments.

As Phoebe wrote each of them down, she felt a sick feeling in her belly.

These judgments seemed to be sentencing her to a lonely, unfulfilled life.

Each of them appeared to be limiting what could ever happen during the decades to come.

Here is what Phoebe found herself writing:

*I am not pretty enough.*

*I am not intelligent enough.*

And the one that really cut to the quick:

*I am unlovable.*

Phoebe knew the next step in the process is to challenge each of these bombshells.

For each of the judgments, she asked herself, "Is this true — for sure?"

The first two judging statements were fairly easy to disprove.

Phoebe decided it was quite possible to find a man who would see her as attractive and intelligent enough to want to get to know.

But the final judgment felt heavy and immovable.

More fear arose.

The mind piped up: *What if I **am** unlovable?*

Then a deeper part of Phoebe began to communicate in its quiet, subtle way.

Her true Self gently reminded her that she has, in fact, been abundantly blessed with love throughout her life.

*My parents love me, and my Aunt Ruth has always treated me with special affection.*

*The patients at the hospital seem genuinely happy to see me when I come around with the library cart.*

*And I have several good friends who seem to find me lovable.*

The belief that *I am unlovable* sounds way less convincing to Phoebe than it seemed just a few minutes ago.

In fact, she can see now that it is not true at all.

Suddenly, the fear that she will never find love seems like a crazy thing to hang on to.

Phoebe decides to turn the whole thing over to the Divine.

She says a little prayer, reads her list of beliefs and judgments aloud, and recognizes that believing them has caused her more than a little suffering.

She feels some grief and sadness about the ways this issue has tied up her life energy for so long.

No wonder she hasn't experienced a satisfying relationship!

Believing that was impossible definitely didn't help it to happen.

But now she knows that can change.

Phoebe turns the fear and all the beliefs that led to it over to Divine Mother, the spiritual presence with whom she feels most connected.

Phoebe then gives thanks and sits for a few minutes in silence, simply being with the shifts she feels taking place within her.

Within minutes, she feels a lightness in her body, along with a sense of hope that has been absent for decades.

Who knows what can happen now?

Phoebe looks forward to finding out.


## Guilt and Shame

When judging goes on, the emotions most frequently present are **guilt** and **shame**.

When we judge ourselves, we feel guilty and ashamed of our own behavior.

When we judge others, we often try to get them to feel guilty or ashamed of themselves.

We manipulate them into feeling bad about themselves by using what has been called a "guilt trip."

Guilt and shame often lie beneath other, more surface emotions.

They reflect a lack of love and acceptance of what is present within us.

Ultimately, guilt and shame suggest a rejection of our very selves.

Feelings of guilt and shame indicate the presence of heavy judgments.

These bottom-line judgments sound like this:

*I'm bad.*

*Maybe I am even evil.*

*There's something wrong with me.*

*I must be defective.*

Guilt and shame are likely to be hidden in the unconscious, where they subtly but pervasively influence our lives.

It is difficult to feel happy and at peace with ourselves and our lives when we wear the overcoats of guilt and shame.

These two emotions stand in the way of happiness for all too many human beings.

As overcoats come off and the Self steps forward ever more fully, we find ourselves judging less.

In the process, we shed the stultifying skins of guilt and shame.

We feel at peace with who and what we are in more and more moments.

And Life has a way of reflecting this newfound inner stillness with outer blessings.

We experience more connection, love, beauty, harmony — the gifts of a life with the Self at its center.

## Slippery Spiritual Judgments

Some of the most painful judgments are the "spiritual" ones.

We compare ourselves to others who seem far superior, and then judge ourselves.

"He seems so enlightened, while I'm nothing but a spiritual laggard."

"I should be further along by now -- I've been on the spiritual path for decades."

"I'm still not able to manifest all the abundance in my life that I want. I'm mired in poverty consciousness."

"I've been working on myself for so long, but I still have all this emotional baggage."

Do you hear the judgments?

In the first two examples, the speakers are judging themselves as spiritually defective.

They may be secretly thinking, *It's hopeless — I'm never going to wake up!*

In the third example, the speaker judges himself as emotionally damaged and defective.

"I'm bad" may be the hidden subtext in all three judging statements.

Spiritual judgments can be the cruelest of all, since so many people on a spiritual path have unrelenting, perfectionistic spiritual standards.

It gets even trickier, since harsh self-judgments are what launched many of us on a spiritual path to begin with.

The resulting pressure to live up to an impossible spiritual ideal can be crushing when we haven't liked our human self very much.

Doesn't it seem ironic that the spiritual quest, something most of us would agree is a positive endeavor, should result in some of the most crippling judgments of all?

Many spiritual teachings counsel loving ourselves and one another, which sounds like the noblest of aspirations.

But the mind can grab even these lofty intentions and use them to beat us up.

"I can't believe how impatient and unloving I can be -- to the very people I love most!"

"I yelled at my kids again this morning, and they were just sitting there eating breakfast. I am such a spiritual failure!"

"How can I think I'm making any spiritual progress at all when I haven't had a decent relationship in twelve years?"

Spiritual judgments negate the awakening that is underway, since it hasn't brought us to the heights of perfection.

We feel justified in trashing ourselves when we believe there is someplace to reach -- a state, a level, a way of being -- that we are nowhere near, in our own estimation.

In the process, we forget that the Self is always and forever holy, pure, and perfect.

Forgetting that we **are** the Self, we transfer the same relentless push to achieve goals that is epidemic in our culture from the workplace to our spiritual lives.

Just as going after impossible heights has led to more than one suicide in the unforgiving work-world, holding ourselves to unreachable standards in our quest for Self-realization constitutes spiritual suicide.

We don't get to celebrate the consciousness openings we've been blessed with when we are busy putting ourselves down for not having more of them.

We belittle ourselves for not having visions complete with dramatic special effects, or hearing wise, eloquent inner voices, or whatever we idealize.

What *is* happening can never measure up to our internalized images of what *should* be going on.

Spiritual judgments form some of the stickiest, most difficult-to-release overcoats of all.

It is hard to float in the ocean of love that is the true nature of things when we refuse to bring that same love to our own journey of awakening.

As long as we exist in a form that is even slightly differentiated from the One Great Being, there will be another step in the journey Home, another iota of separation to transcend.

This is not a problem -- unless we make it one.

It is simply the way it is.

And we are all in this together.

How can anyone be ahead of anybody else when our ultimate destination is floating in Eternity within the infinite All In All?

Who can say where each of us "should" be in that journey?

How can we judge anything about ourselves when we are each a divine, perfect aspect of the One?

There is nothing we could ever achieve that would make us more than what we already are.

All there is to do is to remove the veils that have hidden it from us.

Seen through the eyes of our true Self, we are right on time and exactly where we need to be.

Suddenly, "This shouldn't be happening" and "I'm not doing this right" sound like the most absurd, laughable statements imaginable.

As you laugh, feel the heavy overcoats of judgment sloughing off.

## Fake Feeling Statements — Judgments in Disguise

Many mental concepts are expressed in so-called feeling statements that are actually judgments in disguise.

For instance: "I feel like I don't really take my spiritual life seriously."

Do you hear the judgment in that statement?

Beneath the words, the speaker may be judging herself as insincere or uncommitted.

Hidden within these judgments may lurk even deeper ones, such as *Something is wrong with me* or *I'm not OK*.

Here's another example of a fake feeling statement:

"I feel like everyone else in the workshop 'gets' the teachings, but I don't."

Again, a judgment is masquerading as a so-called feeling statement.

The speaker might feel embarrassed, or anxious, or sad, or frustrated.

But no true feeling is expressed, only comparison and judgment.

The others are judged positively and placed on a pedestal -- they "get" the teachings, while the speaker judges himself as one-down because he doesn't.

It's bad enough to slay ourselves with these judgments masquerading as feelings.

When we make these "fake feeling statements" about others, things can get really confusing.

"I feel like she doesn't mean what she says."

There are undoubtedly feelings present in the speaker, but we have no way of knowing what they are since there is no expression of feeling going on here at all.

What is really meant here: "I am making the judgment that she does not mean what she says."

Consider a third fake feeling statement.

"I feel like he ripped me off — he is a spiritual charlatan."

Again, the speaker is neither in touch with his feelings nor expressing them.

He might feel sad, or disappointed, or full of rage, but he verbalizes only his perception and projection about what happened, followed by a judgment of the other person.

A lot of us have heard the injunction to make feeling statements rather than speak from our heads.

We may have learned to start with "I feel..." and to complete the thought with an actual feeling, like "happy" or "irritated."

This is helpful advice.

It promotes self-awareness and its expression through clear communication.

But as soon as we add "like" to "I feel" we are no longer in feeling territory.

Now we have crossed over into the land of judgment.

Be alert to this phrase in conversation, and in your own inner dialogues, and watch what comes after "I feel like..." followed by a pronoun.

It is almost always a judgment in drag.

It may be trying to pass itself off as a bona fide feeling, but a judgment is always a judgment.

And every judgment, whether of ourselves or someone else, piles on yet another overcoat.

## Releasing Judgment

Reversing the downward spiral of judgments begins with ourselves.

When we can look in a mirror with the eyes of kindness, we start to see others in the same way.

Seeing ourselves as a work in process with no "Complete By" date, we stop going after the unreachable heights of perfection.

This shift makes it easier to accept others as they are, too.

And as we realize that Life is bringing us *only* experiences that serve our awakening, we stop judging them as wrong and bad.

Instead, we open to What Is and explore how we might embrace the situation as a pathway Home.

This is how we stop piling on more overcoats of judgment.

# 22

# Helplessness and Hopelessness

*The question is not what you look at,*
*but what you see.*

*Henry David Thoreau*

As we stop attempting to squelch and censor our feelings and become more comfortable with letting them be what they are, overcoats of self-repression drop away.

Witnessing our thoughts and judgments and realizing not one of them is true helps us to relinquish even more overcoats.

Peeling away the overcoats of suffering by being with what is present in each one, we eventually confront some of the deepest levels of all: helplessness and hopelessness.

We feel *helpless* when we don't know what to do with a feeling or situation, or don't believe we have what it takes to deal with it.

We feel *hopeless* when we do not see any way through it.

Each of these feelings rests on one or more fears.

When *helplessness* is present, we fear we are inadequate to the task of being with What Is.

We fear we are not capable of finding our way through it.

Feelings of *hopelessness* indicate that we fear there simply **is** no way through the situation into a better place.

The only word for how it appears to us is **hopeless**.

Helplessness is more about us, while hopelessness often centers on the situation itself.

But the two frequently coexist and blur together in a quicksand morass of "What's the use?"

Our helpless, hopeless fears can keep us from even looking at the issue, or our feelings about it, if they are strong enough.

It may seem pointless to even try.

The key is to recognize that we are in the grip of potent feelings -- helplessness and hopelessness.

These two feelings can look so convincing that we can find ourselves giving way to them.

They seem utterly real and true.

Depressingly unquestionable.

Listen to how final this sounds: "It's hopeless."

End of story.

Or is it?

When we buy into these two knockout feelings, we go down for the count.

Believing the mind's litany of hopelessness and helplessness has resulted in more suicides than we will ever know.

If we are to survive the process of investigating our emotions, we must learn how to deal with the deepest, most seductively real-looking feelings of them all.

Helplessness and hopelessness are so good at masquerading as The Truth that we may find ourselves bowing at their feet, as if they were great sages or oracles telling us The Way It Is about ourselves, our challenges, and Life itself.

The key lies in remembering that there is *nothing real* about what they are saying.

Hopelessness and helplessness are merely feelings.

Strong ones, to be sure, but still feelings.

Nothing more.

They can only take us down if we buy into them and believe they are true.

At those moments, we need to remind ourselves that only one thing is ultimately real and true -- the divine essence at our core.

Helplessness and hopelessness have nothing to do with That.

Like all other feelings, they are temporary.

They are nothing more than clouds moving through the eternal sky of our being.

They may seem like enormous, dark clouds, but even the fiercest storm eventually passes through.

We need to remember that helplessness and hopelessness, like all other feelings, are overcoats.

They are not who we really are.

That is the last thing they hope we will realize, for then they are busted.

Their jig is up.

When we can **see** the feelings for what they are and **feel** the helplessness and hopelessness, we remember:

*What this feeling is trying to convince me of is not real or true.*

*This is intense, and seems very potent, but it is **just a feeling**.*

*I can breathe into it and feel it, and turn it over to God for help.*

*Just like I do with any other feeling.*

*This one feels big, but I can meet it and greet it just as I do with all the others.*

*Ultimately, this has no truth, no reality, and no power.*

*It only seems that way.*

It is always a good idea to turn over all of our emotions to Something Larger, especially the feelings that seem too strong to deal with ourselves.

We do not need to know what to do with them.

What a relief!

Surrender and the grace of God always offer the ultimate way through.

As awakening humans, we normally tap into only a little of the unlimited power of our true nature.

But when we call to the Divine, we tap into the unlimited transformative power of the One.

While we might compare the light of our little, human consciousness to a 100-watt bulb, through surrender to a higher power we potentially access millions of watts of illumination.

Hopelessness and helplessness want us to believe there is no way through them.

But, like the messages of all other feelings, that is not true.

When hopelessness and helplessness arise, the faster we turn them over to a vaster level of reality, the sooner we will be shown the way through them.

Whenever we feel ourselves sinking, we can remind ourselves to *go vaster, faster.*

Inviting the words to arise on their own, we might find ourselves saying something like:

"Here, God, please take the burden of these feelings from me. I do not know what to do with it all, and it seems so very real. I don't want to believe what the feelings are saying, so please reveal the truth to me."

Then, we can open to the mystery of what the Divine will bring forth.

We might be shown the divine light in our sacred center, the ultimate reminder of who we are and what is possible.

Or we may suddenly see the unreality of what was trying to pass itself off as true.

We may hear the "still, small voice" of the Self whispering simple words of wisdom and comfort to counteract the false testimony of the feelings.

A glimpse of a way through may even show itself to us.

We build spiritual muscle every time we stand up to strong, intense feelings like hopelessness and helplessness without giving way to them.

With each encounter we discover that within us lies the strength that overcomes all challenges -- the limitless power of the Divine.

And should these deep, challenging feelings again arise, we remember to call upon the power of the One sooner, and to turn over the feelings and fears faster.

We do not need to wear these burdensome overcoats for a moment longer.

## The Dark Night

Most of us will probably encounter feelings of helplessness and hopelessness along the way to full awakening.

When we are willing to follow the thread of awareness through whatever arises, we will be led deeper and deeper toward the roots of our suffering, which often lie within these feelings.

When we can be with them, rather than turning away from them, we lessen their power to unconsciously limit our lives.

At times, though, the feelings of hopelessness and helplessness are so strong and convincing that we cannot find a way through them.

They may go away only to return, again and again.

We may find some temporary relief through feeling the feelings and reminding ourselves they are not the truth about us or our life.

But no matter how many times we turn them over to the Divine, before long we feel flattened by the weight of the emotions again.

The overcoats of despair and hopelessness may have become so heavy they do not seem possible to budge.

When this is the case, we have entered into what spiritual writers through the centuries have called the Dark Night.

Now, our journey takes us "through the valley of the shadow of death."

This does not usually refer to our own physical death, unless facing our imminent transition out of the body lies at the core of the Dark Night.

We may, though, find ourselves deeply contemplating the meaning of life in light of the fact that we all leave the earthly plane after but a few decades here.

Mourning the passing of a loved one can also send us into a Dark Night.

During the Dark Night, death can seem like a reasonable, even welcome solution to the challenges we face, which can appear insurmountable.

But the Dark Night is not about seeking escape from our hardships.

Instead of hoping for a way out through physical death, we are being asked to die to who we thought we were.

We may also be forced to let go of parts of our life that are no longer what they once were -- home, job, relationship, health.

Less tangible aspects of our experience might have fled -- satisfaction, creative fulfillment, mental-emotional well-being.

During the Dark Night, thick overcoats of who we are not are brought to our attention.

So many layers of not-Self surface to be released that it can look dark indeed beneath it all.

A dense, impenetrable blanket of storm clouds may seem to completely fill the clear, open sky of our awareness.

The Dark Night feels overwhelming, and we seem to be intensely alone with our suffering.

It can even seem that we are dying, that the process will consume us until there is nothing left of us.

But this, like all ideas, is only an idea.

It is not the truth about what is going on.

Although it can seem as if our very being is dying, what is dying is a *way of being*.

A caterpillar must die to its current reality in order to be reborn as a butterfly.

In a similar way, we are compelled to abandon our small, human identity, even though a part of us desperately wants to hang on to it.

But the only way we can become an entirely new creature, a butterfly who will soar free of all it once believed it was, is to release the old ways of being.

They are too limited now for who we are becoming.

Even parts of us we loved and were proud of, and ways of being that brought approval and outer success, may need to be relinquished.

During these times, it helps to remember the saying, "What looks like death to the caterpillar is birth to the butterfly."

Out of the ashes of all we have known ourselves to be will emerge the magnificent Self that is now ready to come forth.

However, if the feelings of hopelessness are suggesting that returning to a former addiction, or even suicide, would be a good decision, it is time to seek professional help.

The true Self never counsels us to damage or destroy ourselves.

These thoughts and feelings are the last-ditch efforts of our small, limited identity to stay alive, even as it knows it is dissolving and dying.

In the face of such powerful emotion, the utmost self-love and compassion will show us the way through.

It may also be wise to seek out the support of someone capable of helping us through such difficult passages.

We do not need to struggle through our suffering by ourselves.

Some overcoats have been there for so long, and are so heavy, that they may seem like the most real and true things about us.

When, in fact, they are the exact opposite of that.

When we feel confused about what is really real — when we feel overwhelmed with negativity and despair — support from a caring, compassionate professional offers a lifeline, a way through the intensity to a new way of being.


## Summing Up

This section of the book has presented the primary layers of our overcoats.

As we have seen, they are not esoteric or obscure.

Our overcoats are the stuff that earthly life is made up of.

When we haven't known how to deal with what was happening, our unfelt feelings and unchallenged thoughts became woven into our overcoats.

These are the layers that veil the true Self, hiding it from our awareness.

They are the disguises we believe are real, making it hard to remember who we really are.

Now that we know more about what we are wearing, we are ready to learn how to shed these layers of not-Self.

Every time we let an overcoat go, our true Self shines out into the world more brightly.

As we become lighter and freer, our divine essence more radiantly expresses through all that we do and all that we are.

In more and more moments, we live as the Self, not our overcoats.

# PART FOUR

✤ ✤ ✤

# A Simple, Loving Approach to Taking Off Overcoats

✤ ✤ ✤

# 23

# Breathe, Feel, Witness, and Turn it Over to God

*There is only one journey:*
*Going inside yourself.*

*Rainer Maria Rilke*

Now that you have read about the various layers of your overcoats, you may have some questions.

*How do we help our overcoats to release so we can go free?*

*Are there different methods of taking off the various kinds of overcoats we are wearing?*

*Will the process be complicated and hard to remember?*

*Or could it really be as easy as watching brilliantly colored leaves fall from the trees each autumn?*

There are thousands of ways to make overcoat removal difficult and time-consuming.

Entire schools of therapeutic techniques are built around long and involved methods of letting go of what we are not so we can live as who we are.

Some of us have been in therapy or analysis for years, yet may still feel as burdened as we did when we began.

Although we intuit that there must be another way, we do not know how to get there from where we are.

Many of us feel an urgency, an inner compulsion to get free, and a sense that **now is the time**.

Fortunately, taking off overcoats is not meant to be hard or to take forever.

Through grace, our overcoats can fall away as easily as a spring snowfall melts.

We can cut through the complexity and allow the process to be as easy as it wants to be.

Whenever we become aware of an overcoat — whenever we feel less than clear, happy, and loving — a simple process can guide us through the two stages of overcoat removal.

The first step is being with the overcoat — meeting it right where it is.

The second part is letting it go.

This simple process can be summed up like this:

**Breathe, feel, witness, and turn it over to God.**

Let's take this sentence apart and examine each piece.

Bringing our awareness to our **breathing** turns our attention toward our inner world, where all true change begins.

Being willing to **feel** whatever we find there opens up the inner pathways and channels so our life energy can get unstuck and freely move once again.

**Witnessing** all that we come upon within ourselves reminds us that our "stuff" is not who we are — we are the One Who Witnesses, not the distressing appearance of what we perceive.

Admitting we have no idea what to do with any of it means we recognize that is not our job.

All we need to do is surrender it into Something Larger.

We let it all go as we **turn it over** to the Divine.

The next few chapters delve more deeply into each aspect of this process.

They also include guided inner Experiences so you can begin to work with each step.

# 24

# Breathe

*Breathing in, I calm body and mind.*
*Breathing out, I smile.*
*Dwelling in the present moment,*
*I know this is the only moment.*

Thich Nhat Hanh
*Being Peace*

Breath is life energy.

Each time we breathe in, some of the infinite energy of the universe flows into our bodies.

And with each outbreath, some of what we no longer need is carried out of our physical forms to rejoin the Whole.

With each breath, we take in, and let go.

We open to the New, and release the Old.

This sacred transfer of energy goes on many times during each minute we are alive.

Yet our breathing is not something most of us pay any attention to.

Unlike taking a shower or fixing ourselves a meal, we are not "doing" it or making it happen.

Even though we could not live without breathing, we rarely even notice that it is going on.

We are probably unaware of the life-giving infusion each breath brings into us.

We may not be breathing as fully or as often as our bodies would enjoy.

Some of us have endured so much trauma that we live in a state of perpetually holding or limiting our breath, wondering what will go wrong next.

When our breathing is shallow, we aren't receiving the life energy we need to truly thrive and feel our best.

The life within us is less able to exchange energies with the life all around us.

This can lead to feeling disconnected and alone.

When our life force has been muted or shut down, taking in more life-giving energy through the breath can be a radical act.

The breath brings new possibilities for healing and regeneration to all parts of us, on all levels of our being.

Who knows what might happen as we open to those unknown energies and possibilities?

## The Life-giving Grace of the Breath

When breath is present in the body, there is life.

When the soul leaves the body, the life-force carried by the breath goes with it.

This is why the breath is such a powerful way to begin to get in touch with our inner world.

Breath is life.

Feeling the life in us through feeling the breath helps us to become aware of what is happening within, whether it is the experience of an overcoat, or basking in the divine splendor at our core.

The breath provides a bridge from the outer world of the senses and the thinking mind to the inner realms of the true Self.

When we focus awareness on the breath, our consciousness automatically begins to shift away from "out there" and toward "in here."

For thousands of years, yogis and spiritual seekers have worked with the breath to expand consciousness beyond the human mind and all of its preoccupations.

These practices offer enduring testimony to the power of the breath as a tool for awakening.

There are many valuable and time-honored breathing techniques, but the simple process we are going to be using does not include any of them.

Instead, we can put aside everything we've ever learned about the breath and come into the freshness of the present moment.

We'll drop into the space of "don't know" -- the space of beginner's mind -- and see what reveals itself to us.

We're going to do something that practically no one ever does: simply feel the breath as it breathes us, exactly the way it wants to do that.

There is absolutely no way to do this wrong.

In fact, we are not going to be "doing" anything.

All we are going to "do" is let the breath breathe us, and notice whatever we notice as each breath comes and goes.

We are not going to try to change what is going on, or fix anything.

There **is** nothing to change or fix.

Each breath is perfectly fine as it is.

Accepting the breath as it is without trying to fix or change it can help us to accept and allow whatever else is going on within us.

If we can let the breath be as it is, we just might find it easier to let everything else about us be as it is.

Since being with the breath is core to the process of releasing overcoats, the following Experience is longer and more in-depth than most of those to follow.

As you work with this Experience, the facility you gain in being present to your breathing will provide a strong foundation for all the Experiences to come.

## Experience: Being with the Breath

Invite your body to get comfortable.

Alternate reading a few lines of this Experience and then allowing your eyes to gently close so you can feel your awareness turning within.

Become aware of the breath coming into your body and going back out.

You might notice sensations in your nostrils, in the back of your throat, or elsewhere.

*Witness* the breath as it moves in and out.

Observe all the sensations associated with the breath as it comes in and goes back out of the body.

Allow some time to experience being the free witness of all that arises with the breath.

Now bring your awareness into the *feeling* of the breath moving.

Notice the subtle, tactile sensations of the flow of the breath.

You may feel the rising and falling of your chest or belly, or other bodily sensations.

*Witness* the breath moving, then *feel* the sensations.

Let your awareness move back and forth between experiencing the pure witness and then dropping into the kinesthetic experience of the sensations.

Breathe, feel, witness.

You will notice that witnessing and feeling gradually blend into an experience of Witnessing~Feeling.

Feel the breath breathing you in exactly the way it wants to do that.

Each breath is just as it needs to be.

Feel the relaxation that occurs as this realization sinks in.

It is all OK, exactly as it is.

The breath is as it is, perfect in each moment.

From here, it is not such a big stretch to open to the possibility that *I am OK, exactly as I am.*

But this exercise is not about getting busy with an idea.

It is about breathing.

So let's return to feeling each breath come in through the nostrils, go wherever it goes within the body, and then leave.

Feel the tiny sensations at the nostrils, the rush of cool air past the delicate hairs within the nose, the slight whoosh as the breath continues on its way into the body.

One breath may be short and quick, while the next is longer and slower.

Each breath simply is what it is.

A thought may arise that all the breaths should be the same, or that longer, deeper breaths are better than shorter, shallower ones.

But each breath is the way it is, regardless of what the mind may think about it.

Thoughts will come and go, for thinking is what mind does.

There is no point in trying to stop the thoughts from arising.

Simply witness them and invite your awareness to return to the breath.

You may notice judgments, "shoulds," and other ideas about how you are "doing."

But since you are not doing anything, you can let these go by without giving them any power.

Observe the judgments and then return to the breath.

And again sink into the comforting reality that you are being breathed.

You have absolutely no ability to breathe yourself.

Life is breathing you, one breath at a time.

The breath is coming in, and then it is going back out, and there is no one making that happen.

Not even the most talented human being can cause the breath to do what it does.

We can control the breath for limited periods of time, but eventually it will return to doing what it does.

In fact, even if we try to stop breathing entirely, we will eventually gasp for breath or go unconscious, and breathing will automatically resume.

Life is in control.

Sink more deeply into non-doing and go free.

Quiet moments of simply feeling~witnessing the breath may be followed by more thoughts.

You may have dropped into letting the breath be as it is, when an idea like "I should be breathing more deeply" suddenly arises.

Notice what the mind is saying, then return to the breath, exactly the way it is breathing you.

Any attempt to make the breath be a certain way would be efforting, and this is not about effort.

Another thought may arise: "There's something wrong with the way I am breathing."

Or a question: "Shouldn't more be happening than this?"

The mind may insist there is something urgent you need to do right away.

No matter what arises, all you need to do is one thing.

Return to the breath, feeling the breath come in and go back out.

One breath at a time.

And remember, you are not doing the breathing.

Life is.

And how can we improve upon Life itself?


## Reflection:

What was it like for you to be present with your breathing?

What did you notice?

Was this a comfortable experience, or did discomfort arise?

Were you aware of feelings or thoughts coming and going along with the breath?

Did the mind kick in with ideas or questions?

What else happened or didn't happen?

As always, the most helpful attitude is to hold it all in love and acceptance.

The breath is something you will return to many, many times as you continue to journey into full awakening.

Being with the breath is one of the most powerful and effective ways to get in touch with your deeper, true Self.

It is also just as helpful in discovering the overcoats that are obscuring your inner radiance, and letting them go.

You might like to incorporate this practice into your daily quiet time with yourself.

Sitting quietly for even a few minutes each morning can set the tone for your day and begin it on a note of self-intimacy.

When you begin your day by getting in touch with yourself, your activities and relationships are more likely to reflect the love and clarity of your true Self.

You are less likely to lose touch with your own energy and truth throughout the day if it has begun with some time to be with yourself.

Journalling about bringing awareness to your breath offers a way to articulate and then reflect on your experiences.

Over time, your journal entries will chronicle your ever-expanding awareness of your inner world.

You might like to experiment with setting aside some time each morning or evening to sit quietly and be with your breath.

Then journal, even briefly, about what that was like.

## The Gift of Breath-Awareness

Being with the breath is a basic practice that enhances your ability to remain here and now.

The key lies in noticing when your awareness moves away from the breath to a thought or feeling, and then gently inviting it to return to your breath.

Over time, the length of time during which you are able to stay focused on the breath will expand, and the mind will correspondingly pull on your awareness less and less.

Occasionally a mind-storm might arise.

Or an itch, a pain, or a noise in the room might clamor for your attention.

Whatever the challenge, the recommended response is the same:

Notice what is present and return awareness to the breath.

This is how you free your awareness from the grip of outer distractions of the mind and senses.

During daily life, we are largely unaware of how often we get caught up in the thinking mind.

Notice the way the simple act of paying attention to your breathing brings all of your awareness within your own self.

As you observe and feel your breath, you soon become aware of how often your awareness drifts into thoughts and loses track of witnessing and feeling the breath.

Through bringing awareness back to the breath, over time the mind-chatter naturally subsides, because the energy of your attention is no longer fueling it.

Being with the breath is perhaps the simplest way of experiencing intimacy with yourself.

You are being with you -- no one else is involved, and nothing else needs to be brought into the experience.

Focusing on the breath is a way of giving yourself the gift of sacred time and space.

There is nothing to do, nothing to strive toward, no goal at all other than being present with yourself.

As you patiently observe and feel the breath, amidst the variety of sensations and thoughts that come and go, you will notice moments when it seems that nothing is going on.

You drop into a stillness and peace rarely encountered in our busy, outer-focused lives.

When breathing and feeling is all that remains in your awareness, even the witness may dissolve, until all that remains is pure awareness -- pure being itself.

Bask in the stillness.

When the mind wanders, simply return your awareness to the breath and feel the sensations that accompany it.

Over time, the quiet gaps between sensations, thoughts, and feelings will grow longer.

Savor these glimpses of the peace of the Self.

They are showing you your own true nature.


## Breath Awareness in Daily Life

As you practice bringing your awareness to your breathing, you may begin to notice that breath awareness also occurs throughout daily life.

Standing in line at the grocery store or washing the dishes, you suddenly feel the sensations of the breath coming and going.

In that instant, you are swiftly and effortlessly brought back into connection with your inner world.

You can also choose to deliberately incorporate breath awareness throughout the day.

Arriving at a stoplight while driving, you close your eyes for an instant and turn your awareness inward to your breathing, feeling each breath coming in and going back out.

During a break at work or before getting out of the car to do an errand, you pause for a few moments and feel your breath breathing you.

This simple practice can reset your energy and even restart your day.

No matter what is going on in the outer world, giving yourself the gift of a quiet, inner moment provides a respite from outer stresses and challenges.

At any moment, you can visit an oasis of peace within you in which everything is fine, just as it is.

The sense of intimacy with yourself that following the breath brings is not dependent upon being alone.

It can happen anywhere -- sitting on a bus, walking down a busy street, in the midst of a meeting.

*Ah, here is the breath, my constant companion.*

*Here I am with myself once again. How good it is to be back!*

Over time, these moments weave together to strengthen your overall sense of peace.

Dropping into your inner world of awareness many times throughout the day creates a harmonious fabric of coherence that, over time, gradually replaces the tangled threads of worry and anxiety, chaos and confusion.

There is a reason so many spiritual practices center on awareness of the breath.

This simple act has tremendous power to change our experience of ourselves.

When the world "out there" seems to be bombarding us with stimulation, we can return to ourselves whenever we like through becoming aware of our breathing, which opens the door to our inner world.

Being conscious of our breathing can shift us from reacting to outer events to allowing responses to arise from a quiet, inner space of stillness.

Being aware of the breath also loosens up our overcoats.

Simply put, overcoats are accumulations of energy, patterns of thought and feeling that have become repetitive reactions to life events.

Overcoats carry energy that is no longer freely flowing.

To one degree or another, it has become dammed-up, stuck and frozen in place.

This is why overcoats feel heavy and burdensome.

When life energy is moving, we feel light and airy.

As it stops flowing and accumulates, we feel dense and thick.

When breathing joins with awareness, the life-force in the breath energizes these stuck places within us, and they begin to move and flow again.

We breathe spaciousness into the layers that have accumulated, and they start to decompress.

Air circulates among the layers, replacing staleness with the freshness of a basket of clean laundry that has dried beneath an azure sky.

The simple act of breathing with awareness allows old, stagnant energy to release, opening things up and inviting new energy to pour into us.

Breath-awareness is central to overcoat-awareness.

And breathing with awareness helps overcoats that are ready to release to more easily and effortlessly drop away.

# 25

# Feel Sensations

*Who looks outside, dreams.*
*Who looks inside, awakes.*

*Carl Jung*

When you became aware of your breathing during the Experience in the previous chapter, you also became aware of feeling.

We feel many kinds of bodily sensations, like itches and aches.

We also feel a variety of emotions ranging from subtle sadness to intense anger.

This chapter deals with feeling body-sensations. The next is about feeling emotions.

As we drop into our breath and our awareness turns inward, the first thing we feel tends to be the variety of sensations in the physical body.

Bodily sensations form the first layer of our overcoats.

And they are also often present within all other layers of overcoats.

Therefore, cultivating awareness of body-sensations serves to help all the layers of our overcoats to release.

## Releasing Bodily Contraction

A place in the body with recurring pain or discomfort is alerting us to an underlying energetic contraction.

Inviting the breath into a painful or numb place in the body can help the contracted area to expand and take up all the room it needs to flourish again.

Breath by breath, we feel the contraction relax and spread back out.

This is how we help our bodies to open back up to the flow of life, no matter how severe the traumas of the past may have been.

You have already experienced bringing awareness to your breathing.

Now, it's time to add bodily sensations to the mix.

The following Experience presents a simple practice to cultivate awareness of them.

Just as with the breath, becoming aware of body-sensations is core to the process of shedding overcoats.

The facility you develop with these fundamental Experiences will carry over into all the other Experiences in this book.

The more comfortable you become with bringing awareness to the breath and to the sensations in your body, the easier it becomes for overcoats to slough off.

## Experience: Feeling Body-Sensations

PART ONE: Whole-body Breathing

Invite your body to come into a comfortable position, preferably sitting up with your spine straight.

Alternate reading these directions and closing your eyes to turn your awareness inward.

Become aware of your breathing, just as you did during the previous chapter's Experience.

Witness and feel the breath breathing you, one breath followed by the next.

Notice any sensations related to the breath.

You may feel your lungs inflating and then deflating as the breath comes in and goes back out.

You belly may rise and fall with the breath.

You might feel moving air tickling your nostrils as each breath enters your nose.

Now, let your awareness expand to progressively include the rest of your body.

Give each area all the time it wants.

First, follow your awareness down into your chest.

Observe the breath moving in and our of your chest and become aware of any sensations associated with the breath or arising within the chest.

When that feels complete for now, invite the breath to travel down your arms.

Witness and feel any sensations in your arms.

Now, invite the breath and your awareness to move up through your neck and into your head.

Feel the breath bringing more space into your neck and head, where so much tension is often stored.

Witness whatever you find and breathe into it, feeling the sensations that are present.

Next, invite the breath to go into your abdomen.

Feel your breath flowing all through your abdominal area and notice any sensations present there.

Witness and feel the sensations arising in your belly, where tightness tends to accumulate.

As you continue to breathe into the abdomen, you may feel a welcome softening taking place there.

When that feels complete for now, invite your breath to flow down into your legs.

As you breathe into your legs, become aware of any sensations in them.

When that feels complete, invite your breath to flow into your entire body.

Feel the unification of all parts of your physical form as you breathe into them simultaneously.

Every aspect of your body is now floating in a unified field of consciousness.

Let yourself enjoy the sensations of unity for as long as you like.

PART TWO: Being More Fully with Sensations

Begin by once again inviting your breath to flow into your entire body.

Feel your physical form floating within a field of energy -- *your* energy.

Within that physical-energetic field, sensations rise up and are present for a time.

Then they fall away, and the next sensation appears.

As you continue to be aware of each breath, notice any new sensations that are present.

You might observe a throbbing in your head, aching in the belly, a tightening in your throat, or something else.

Simply be with whatever is happening.

Now, with the next breath, invite the breath to travel toward the sensation.

Feel the breath moving into it.

Feel the sensation, breath by breath.

You might find that as you feel the first sensation you become aware of for a few breaths, it gives way to another one somewhere else in the body.

Follow your awareness into this new experience and invite the breath to accompany you into the new sensation.

Breathe and feel whatever is present.

After a few breaths, this, too, may dissolve into yet another new sensation.

Follow the trail wherever it takes you.

Feeling the breath, feeling the sensation.

Sometimes, sensations grow stronger before they dissolve.

This is not a sign that anything is wrong.

This place in your body may be asking for more attention and acceptance before it can relax and let go of its tension and contraction.

You may need to stay with the process for a while longer before it releases.

If the sensations become uncomfortably strong or painful, you may want to step back into *witnessing* the sensations instead of dropping into them and feeling them fully.

Observing the pain brings consciousness into it.

Most of the time, this increased awareness helps the underlying contraction to spread out and release, allowing you to more easily feel the sensations.

This locus of challenging sensations may be asking for love and compassion.

It may be a place that has stored painful memories and their associated feelings for a long time.

Embracing whatever is there with full acceptance will help any resistance stored in that part of your body to release.

Melting through resistance means shifting from *NO, I do not want to see or feel what is there* to *YES, I am willing to face and even embrace all that is present within me, one step at a time.*

Releasing resistance means accepting What Is, even if it may be painful or challenging to face and feel.

Follow the trail of sensations for as long as you like, or until the cycle feels complete for now.

## Reflection:

What was it like to be with bodily sensations in this way?

Is this a new practice, or something that feels familiar?

What have you discovered about your capacity to be with whatever is present?

Did you experience any resistance or discomfort with the process itself?

Journalling about your experiences brings even more awareness to what it is like to breathe and feel bodily sensations.

Over time, your journal will record your growing ability to be with What Is.

You might like to devote time each morning or evening to the practice contained in this Experience.

This will increase your capacity to be present with whatever is arising in your inner world.

This practice is also fundamental to all of the Experiences yet to come in this book.


## Lack of Feeling and Numbness

Some of us find that when we begin to breathe into the body with awareness, it seems as if nothing is going on.

No feeling-sensations are present.

It's as though we're breathing into a void.

A null zone.

The mind may object to the whole thing: *Nothing is happening. Why are we doing this? It's a waste of time.*

When numbness and lack of feeling are present, at some time in the past it was probably too painful or uncomfortable to be with what was going on.

We didn't know what to do, so we shut down.

We may have vacated the premises long ago.

Many people who were molested as children talk of "leaving" their bodies and rising up to a safer, more comforting level of reality during the abuse.

This is an understandable strategy when it seems impossible to either physically stop what is happening or leave the situation.

Decades later, the residue of that painful time often persists in bodily numbness, a sure sign of shut-down energy.

Whole parts of our bodies may feel like our mouth does when we get novocaine at the dentist.

Try as we might, we can't feel anything in our lips, tongue, and cheeks.

At the dentist, being numb is a good thing.

In our lives, years after a traumatic event led us to numb ourselves, it is not as helpful.

Bodily numbness is an overcoat of adaptation to unacceptable, if not unbearable circumstances.

Whatever we would rather not feel -- whatever we fear will hurt too much to feel -- goes numb.

Beneath the lack of bodily sensation, the emotions we could not feel at the time are waiting for us to return to them.

They are waiting for the light of consciousness to shine into them and bring healing.

Most of all, they are waiting for love and acceptance.

The mind may tell us it's no use to try.

It may convince us that it's too late, too much has happened, it's too hard to go back to that painful time and revisit what happened then.

*Better to be numb than to hurt.*

But that only binds up our life energy and makes us feel half-alive.

As with so much the mind insists is true, there is no validity to these theories.

At the right moment in our journey of awakening, our awareness will gently, lovingly enter into the areas of the body that have shut down and gone numb.

The empathy and compassion of the true Self will enfold all the places within us where old hurts still live.

As we begin to tenderly face and embrace what lies within us, we shed overcoats of suffering we thought we'd be wearing for the rest of our lives.

## The Importance of Feeling Sensations

Like bringing awareness to the breath, feeling the sensations that are present in the physical body invites us to be intimate with our own experience.

Bringing awareness into bodily sensations also helps our bodies to let go of any tensions and energetic contractions that have developed in response to the stresses of living on Earth.

Working with this practice over time can help you to experience life in a much more fluid, malleable way.

This is especially true if you tend to find being in a body uncomfortable, or if you feel as though you've been walking around within a suit of armor.

When congestion and contraction release, challenging sensations often transform into enjoyable feelings of ease, relaxation, and spaciousness.

As we grow more comfortable feeling the sensations that are present, the mind's tendency to label them subsides.

Increasingly, sensations are not judged as "pleasant" or "unpleasant" -- they simply are what they are.

And we are able to meet them and be with them, regardless of their nature.

Through breathing and feeling sensations, we realize that everything that goes on within us, as well as all that happens in the "outer" world, is merely part of an ever-changing, passing show.

Bringing awareness to the breath and inviting it into sensations within the body renews and revivifies all of the body's systems and organs with the life-giving vital force of the breath.

Thus, inviting congestion and contraction to release can only benefit our health and well-being.

Bringing awareness into bodily sensations and feeling them dissolve helps these layers of our overcoats to become more permeable and porous.

Now, light can filter through the layers that were once dense and opaque.

The essence of our true Self can shine out into the world more and more brightly.

When it seems silly to spend precious time breathing and feeling, we can remind ourselves that this is why we do it.

We are shedding our overcoats so our innermost divine Self can bless the world with its radiance.

Could there be anything more important than that?

# 26

# Feel Emotions

*The only alchemist that turns everything into gold is love.*

*Anais Nin*

During the previous chapter's Experience, you might have noticed that right behind or within the physical sensations you experienced were emotions such as disappointment and impatience.

Emotions are the next layer we encounter when we turn our awareness within.

Now, in addition to feeling the sensations of the breath and sensations elsewhere in the body, we will be present with whatever is going on emotionally.

Moving toward our feelings, not away from them, may seem strange and unfamiliar.

It may be opposite to everything we have learned, and go against all the ways we've been conditioned to respond when feelings arise.

If going toward our feelings is not something we are used to doing, it may take time to become comfortable with this.

That's all right.

It's OK, too, if being with your feelings feels scary.

That might mean it is not yet time to go into the feelings.

It may also mean that it is time to face the fear itself, and not let it stop you.

Susan Jeffers once wrote a book with the wonderful title *Feel the Fear and Do It Anyway.*

That is good advice for all of us who are exploring what lies within our overcoats.

We will encounter many layers that seem daunting to approach.

We may fear that if we start to feel the emotions buried within us, we will be overwhelmed, swept away in a torrent of emotion that has no end.

Some of us fear we will become nonfunctional if we ever begin to go near those feelings.

Will our lives fall apart?

Or will others decide we are crazy and out of control?

If the ideas behind these fears were true, it certainly would make no sense to go anywhere near our feelings.

But are they?

Some trepidation is normal when we are doing something new.

It can help to remember that we do not need to know what to do with what we find.

All we need to do is breathe, feel, witness, and turn it over to the Divine.

But if strong fear arises at the thought of being present to your innermost feelings, read this chapter, if you like, but do not attempt the Experience until you feel ready.

Love yourself and know that your divine Self will bring the feelings that you are ready to face to your attention as you are ready to feel them.

Professional assistance can provide the support necessary for you to feel safe enough to delve into the feelings that remain from past traumas, or that accompany present challenges.

## Welcoming our Feelings

Some feelings may have been waiting a very long time for us to be ready to be with them.

At the time they first arose, they may have been too intense and overwhelming for us to fully feel them.

We may also have received messages that our feelings were not OK.

A parent might have shouted, "You have no right to be angry!"

Or said, "Quit complaining or I'll give you something to complain about!"

A teacher may have shamed us in front of the class when we cried.

For one good reason or another, our feelings went underground to a safe place where they could simmer undisturbed.

There probably isn't a human being who doesn't have some unfelt feelings deep inside.

As we awaken, we become aware of the feelings we have not been ready to feel until now.

The light at our core begins to shine into the dark, hidden places where the feelings have been stored.

The mechanisms we have used to keep them down no longer work.

Eating. Drinking. Smoking. Drugs. TV. Overworking. Overshopping.

It is time for the feelings to be felt, and nothing will keep them down any longer.

At first, they may seem overwhelming.

We fear that if we start to cry, we may cry forever.

Or there may be so much anger boiling up, we feel afraid of what might happen if it spills out of us.

It can seem like a much better idea to keep it all bottled up.

At least then it won't hurt anything or anyone.

But when we bottle up our feelings, the flow of our life energy is likewise dammed up.

We feel stuck.

Our life stalls out.

We wonder why it is that no matter what we try, things are at a standstill.

If this goes on long enough, the life energy that isn't able to move freely becomes congested.

This can form the basis for chronic physical conditions.

Those unfelt feelings are not only a backlog that impedes or stops the flow of our life energy.

They also cloud our ability to be fully present with what is happening right now.

Our stored, unresolved feelings can intensify our emotional responses to what is currently going on.

We sob while watching a sad movie.

A minor slight sends us into a major reaction.

All of this is telling us that something from the past is seeking to be loved, allowed, and most of all, felt.

To make it safe for these stored feelings to arise into our awareness, we need to open up a space of love and acceptance.

There is nothing we need to hold outside this energy-field of allowance and compassion.

When every kind of feeling -- from embarrassment and shame to rage and deep grief -- feels welcome at last, it will come into our awareness and be what it is.

Our only job is to be with it, to say YES to it, and offer it the warm embrace it has been waiting for since it originally arose.

This is how we develop the capacity to be present with whatever is going on.

It is how we stop running away from our feelings -- and ourselves.

When we acknowledge what went on in the past, we can begin to feel the feelings that are still present from those earlier events.

In this way, we reverse the tendency to deny or ignore what is going on within us.

This is how we get unstuck, so something new can happen.

Shedding the overcoats of the past allows us to be more fully here in the present.

## A New Way to Be with Feelings

When "stuff" arises, it is usually in response to what someone else did or said.

We often make it about them: "If s/he hadn't done or said that, I wouldn't be upset."

But the real issue isn't what that person did or said -- it's the anger, fear, sadness, or other feelings that are going on *inside of us.*

Often, we aren't in touch with what is going on in our inner world.

We're not aware that when that person said what s/he said, we felt sad and disappointed, for instance.

All we are aware of is the surface emotion that fuels our reaction.

In this case, that might be a hot fire of anger, expressed as: "How dare s/he say that to me?!"

We aren't acknowledging what is going on deep within -- the more vulnerable feelings of sadness and disappointment.

So how do we prevent ourselves from unconsciously reacting to outer stimuli, which almost always makes the situation worse, and get back in touch with what we're actually feeling?

No matter what appears to be going on "out there," when we turn our attention to our breath, we get back in touch with our inner world -- the only place true healing and change can ever happen.

So, we feel each breath.

And we feel the sensations in our body.

A throbbing here, a clenching there, a hot glob of energy somewhere else.

Or deadness, or heaviness, or a thousand other sensations, all part of the human condition.

We breathe, we feel, we allow.

We're not trying to make anything happen.

We're not doing this so the feeling will go away.

We do this because we love ourselves and we want to give ourselves the most precious gift of all — full presence with whatever IS, moment to moment.

This is all about intimacy, which, as someone clever once pointed out, can be interpreted as *Into Me See*.

Seeing into ourselves makes all the difference when it comes to being with our feelings and not projecting them onto others.

As we feel what is present, the breath becomes our life-line.

Whenever we are feeling overwhelmed by feelings, we can return our awareness to our breath and it will keep us afloat, even in the biggest tsunami of emotion.

We breathe, and we feel, and we soon notice that as we bring awareness to each sensation, letting it fully be what it is, at some point it gives way to the next sensation, and the next.

A hot fire beneath the rib cage may feel like anger, even rage.

We breathe into it and simply feel it, without trying to figure out why it is there or what to do about it.

We stay with it, whether for a few breaths or a few minutes of conscious breathing into what is there.

We stay with this until something new happens.

And then we are present with that.

Suddenly, we become aware that the intensity in the solar plexus has subsided, and now we are aware of a tightness and constriction in the throat.

As we breathe into it and feel the physical sensations, we realize the feeling of fear is also present.

Fear of saying what we really feel.

Fear of expressing ourselves.

Fear we will be punished or even killed if we speak out.

Fear of what other fears might emerge if we keep breath-ing into the throat.

Thoughts may arise: *Wait a minute -- this is intense!*

*Maybe this isn't such a good idea after all.*

We aren't at all sure we have what it takes to meet this intensity, but we decide to continue to stay with what is present, and breathe into it.

We also realize we don't have to jump into the deep end of the pool of feelings.

We can wade in up to our ankles, or our knees, or however far we can go and still comfortably be present to the emotional charge.

If it gets too intense, we can always get out of the pool.

Sometimes we need a while to sit at the edge and observe the feelings from a safe distance.

It might feel too scary to merge with the feelings right away.

In time, after we've spent some time in the shallow end of the pool of feelings, we'll be ready to swim into the deep end and feel whatever is there.

## One Feeling at a Time

Breath by breath, we are getting to know what lies within ourselves.

Some of it is fairly recent, and some of it has been there for a long time.

Returning to the example in the previous section, imagine you are feeling a tightness in your throat.

As you breathe into the throat and the constriction there, breath by breath, it begins to loosen and dissipate.

After some time, you notice it is gone.

Now, imagine that your attention is shifting to a feeling of emptiness in your belly.

Breathing into this new place, you notice the sensation of an inner hollowness, which opens to reveal an ancient sadness deep in the belly.

You remind yourself that all you need to do is stay with what is happening.

Tears well up and spill over.

No idea what this sadness is about, or where it came from.

All you need to do is feel the feeling.

Breathe and feel...breathe and feel.

You continue to follow the invisible thread wherever it takes you.

Sometimes you "get" something about what you find.

A flash of insight or understanding arises, revealing something about the source or the deeper story of the feeling.

At other times, the feeling simply is what it is, with no explanation attached.

It's fine either way.

Everything is revealed on a need-to-know basis.

If you're not getting anything about it, you must not need to know right now.

Trust the process and be at peace.


## Where Feeling Emotions Takes Us

When any of us follows the thread of what is present all the way, it eventually empties out all the feelings that want our attention right now.

At that point, we find ourselves in a state of "nothing going on" — otherwise known as peace.

Stillness.

We could also call it *full availability to the present moment.*

There's no backlog, nothing we're bringing with us from the past into this moment.

That allows this moment to be all it can be.

Enjoy the stillness.

Sink into the peace.

Some call this freedom.

A taste of liberation.

This is why we breathe and feel.

The simplest actions sometimes offer the greatest gifts.

In earlier Experiences, you practiced bringing awareness to your breathing, as well as breathing into, witnessing and feeling bodily sensations.

When we begin to bring awareness to our inner world in this way, the latent emotions held within those sensations and parts of the body are energized and activated.

They've always been there, but they were buried and subconscious.

The subtler realms of our experience begin to come forward into our awareness when we invite the breath and the witnessing~feeling consciousness into our inner world.

To help our overcoats to come off, we need to be willing to feel the pain that is in them.

This is the pain we couldn't fully feel at the time the original event occurred.

This Experience is designed to open up a safe space in which the realm of emotion can be present.

## Experience: Being Fully Present with Emotions

To begin, find a comfortable position for your body, one it can maintain for a while.

As in the previous Experiences, you can alternate reading a few lines and going within to experience them.

Or, read these directions now, and refer back to them during the Experience as needed.

Let your eyes close and witness the breath moving in and out of your body.

Feel your awareness returning to your inner landscape.

Witness the breath for a few moments, and then drop into feeling the sensations of the breath.

Sense the oneness of breathing, witnessing, and feeling as you experience the breath breathing you.

You might feel sensations related to the breath, as well as other sensations in various places in your body.

Allow a few moments to be with whatever is unfolding.

As you become aware of a sensation somewhere in your body, breathe into it and feel what is there.

Then ask if there is an emotion within the sensation, ready to be met and felt.

As the feeling emerges into your awareness, invite the breath into it and feel what is present.

Simply breathe and feel.

No need to do anything with what is arising -- just feel it.

It is what it is.

When there is no resistance to an emotion, as it is allowed and felt, it releases.

You may sense it losing energy and dissolving.

Sometimes, as we meet a feeling, it grows stronger, especially if it has been waiting for some time to be acknowledged and felt.

If this occurs, you can invite your breath and awareness into the outer layers of the intensity.

Breathe and feel, always moving from the periphery inward.

If you've been able to feel some of the emotion and sense it is OK to go further, invite your breath to carry your awareness toward the center of the feeling sensations.

Go at your own pace and slow down whenever the feelings become stronger than is comfortable.

Give yourself a lot of empathy for being willing to feel this long-buried emotion.

A particularly strong emotion may not move through and dissolve right away.

If a feeling seems too strong to stay with, step back and simply witness it, as though you are watching a movie.

In time, the energetic charge of the feeling may subside, allowing you to drop into feeling the emotion.

The feeling may also need more acceptance and compassion from you before it has received what it needs.

Whatever the emotion, you can meet it with empathy and caring.

You can also give yourself empathy for going through the challenging experiences that resulted in the painful feelings you are now uncovering.

Feeling is a sacred messenger from parts of your being and aspects of your experience that want to be loved and included within your totality.

Some feelings may have waited for a long time, deep within, to be invited into the fold.

Be gentle with yourself as you make a place at the table for the feelings that have waited for that invitation.

This is tender, vulnerable territory, to be explored spaciously and patiently, without hurry or force.

All will be revealed -- all will be resolved -- in its own timing.

And at every stage of the journey, you are fine, just as you are.

## Reflection:

Opening to the inner world of feelings is something like donning a snorkel mask and fins.

Looking into the underwater world, we realize there are all kinds of things going on that we never would have known about, had we continued to paddle around on the surface.

When we make ourselves available to our feelings, we discover an entire ocean-full of experiences going on just beneath the surface of our awareness.

As we stop to breathe and feel whatever is present, we may be amazed by the richness and aliveness we discover within ourselves.

Journalling provides a safe, private container for whatever is emerging into your awareness as your inner world of feelings reveals itself to you.

It can also feel nurturing to share what you are discovering about your feeling-world with a trusted friend.

# 27

# Witness

*Look within.*
*Within is the fountain of good,*
*and it will ever bubble up,*
*if thou wilt ever dig.*

*Marcus Aurelius Antoninus*

For most human beings, feeling emotions is a powerful experience.

When we let ourselves feel the sadness, grief, anger, and other emotions present within ourselves, we tend to identify with them.

Thus, we humans often believe that *our emotions are us.*

This tendency to merge with our emotions can cause feelings to be seen as overwhelming and scary, which is why so many of us have pockets of emotion within us that we have never gone near.

Any time we get too involved with what is going on in our lives, it is helpful to stand back and view the situation from a more detached perspective.

This is especially true when we are dealing with feelings.

**Witnessing** an emotion allows us to stand back from it and see it as something that is going on within us, rather than something that we are.

Now, we can form a relationship with the emotion, rather than getting lost within it, thinking we *are* it.

*Ah*, we realize, *this feeling is **what I am experiencing** — it isn't **who I am.***

Witnessing our feelings helps us to bring consciousness to them.

And consciousness is a primary facet of who we really are.

In fact, consciousness is the fundamental nature of the true Self.

Each of us, as a soul, has entered into human life to experience what is only possible here, within this dimension of reality.

One of the most potent experiences available to us here is feeling.

We have the opportunity on Earth to explore a wide range of emotions, from the extremes of angry outrage to the subtlest sensations of awe.

Awakening is not about *eliminating* feeling.

This would be like wiping out the unique colors and scents of all the flowers in a garden.

How dull it would be to walk through such a lifeless place!

Instead, awakening is about *bringing awareness* into the realm of feeling.

And nothing is more helpful in that endeavor than cultivating the ability to witness what is going on, rather than get lost and enmeshed in it.

When we witness what is present, we are standing in the Self.

The Self is the witness.

Witnessing is being fully present with whatever is there.

When we witness a feeling, we can be with it without attempting to do anything with it.

We see even the most challenging feelings for what they are.

Resting in the Witness-Self, we see the truth:

*This is just fear, or loneliness, or anger.*

*It has no power over who I am.*

We may get caught up in it temporarily, but then we return to being the One Who Watches.

This back-and-forth, in-and-out movement is the dance of awakening.

The Witness-Self has no need to try to make anything other than it is, to analyze it, or to judge it.

Witnessing allows us to objectively observe what is present.

For instance, when we notice a fear is present, we might say, "I am feeling fear."

Or: "I am in the experience of fear."

Do you hear the difference between these statements and this common way of expressing emotion: "I am afraid"?

When we put it this way, we qualify the sacred essence of our being, most simply expressed as I AM, with whatever we are feeling.

This reinforces the tendency to *identify* with our emotions, to believe they are *who we are.*

Resting in the Witness-Self, we know that we are not the fear.

It, like everything else, is merely another experience passing through the field of our awareness.

As we see it for what it is, there is nothing to stop it from continuing on.

Which leaves us in the peace of who we truly are.


## Feeling~Witnessing

As awakening progresses, we find ourselves simultaneously feeling whatever is present as well as witnessing it.

Feeling and witnessing merge and blend into *feeling~witnessing*.

We are both experiencing what is present and watching the experience unfold.

For example, when we bring awareness to our breathing, we are feeling the breath and also witnessing the feeling of the breath.

We are feeling the subtle sensations of the breath, while watching each breath come and go.

When physical sensations arise, we can feel them as well as observe them.

We might language this as, "I feel a pain in my elbow I am also witnessing the sensations of that pain."

Or: "I am feeling~witnessing a pain in my elbow."


## Witnessing Overcoats

It bears repeating that, in the mysterious realm of quantum physics, the *mere presence* of an observer has been shown to change the outcome of an experiment.

The same is true in our own inner world.

Once something is observed, it never remains the same.

Whether it is a thought, a feeling, a bodily sensation, or a traumatic memory, once we see it as it is, it never has the same power over us.

This is just as true in the larger context of our lives.

As we develop the capacity to observe, through the eyes of the Self, the ongoing experiment we call life on Earth, we change what can happen.

Bringing consciousness to anything shifts it, and shifts our relationship to it.

When we see something as it is, we eventually see that it is transitory.

It has no ultimate reality.

Like a cloud drifting through the clear blue sky, it is part of the passing show.

Even the most troubling emotion or the most limiting story about who we are has no lasting reality whatsoever.

Overcoats are, by definition, the layers of who we are not.

They are the myriad disguises that try to convince us they are who we really are.

But, like clouds, there is nothing permanent or solid about them.

Overcoats are woven of the contents of the unconscious.

They stay in place as long as we are unaware of what they contain.

As we bring consciousness to our overcoats, they can never remain as heavy and solid as they once seemed.

Eventually, when enough of the light of awareness shines into our overcoats, they dissolve.

This illustrates the enormous power of consciousness.

Witnessing brings the unconscious contents of our over-coats into the conscious realm.

As we see our overcoats for what they are, we dis-identify with them.

We no longer believe they are who we are.

Now, we are able to stand back from them.

We are no longer merged and identified with our over-coats.

This allows us to more fully know who we *really* are — the true Self.

## The Self is the Witness

Being able to witness what is present means that we are identifying with the true Self.

For it is the Self that does the witnessing.

Only the true Self has the capacity to see things as they are.

As we increasingly *know* that we are the Self, we are less and less overwhelmed by the burden of our overcoats.

Standing in the Self ever more fully gives us a new and welcome perspective on our overcoats.

Suddenly, they do not seem nearly as heavy and oppres-sive.

This new awareness helps the layers of not-Self fall away more easily and effortlessly.

Looking at the contents of our overcoats, we know they have nothing to do with who we really are.

The more deeply we know this, the more easily the over-coats drop away.

And the less we are bothered by those that remain, for we know they will release when there is nothing left holding them in place.

Resting in the Self that we are, we are in touch with the infinite intelligence of the Divine.

That intelligence knows everything about everything.

When the contents of an overcoat arise and initially seem frightening and overwhelming, all we need to do is remember who we are.

Even the biggest wave of fear has no power over us now.

For we know that fear is not who we are.

In fact, fear has no resemblance whatsoever to our true nature.

It is witnessing that shows us the difference.

As we witness all that we are not, we rest more fully in who we truly are.

And even the strongest tsunami of emotion can never wash that away.


## Experience: Witnessing

Alternate reading a few lines of these directions and going within to be with what is there.

Begin by once again becoming aware of your breathing.

Feel the breath breathing you, exactly as it wants to do that.

Invite the body sensations and emotions that were present in the previous Experiences to come into your awareness.

Feel them.

Now, step back into being the Witness.

*Observe* whatever is present.

See it all from the viewpoint of the Self that you are.

Notice what you are aware of as the Witness-Self.

From this vantage-point, what can you see about your overcoats?

Can you sense their energetic texture or pattern?

Do you notice anything about them that you weren't previously aware of?

As you witness, is it easier to remember the sensations and feelings are transitory phenomena, not solid reality?

Does resting in the Witness-Self help you to see that they are separate from and external to the core of your true Self?

Feel the difference between resting in the Self and identifying with the contents of your overcoats.

## Reflection:

What was it like to observe the overcoats instead of feeling them?

When the realm of the feelings becomes overwhelming or frightening, stepping back into the Witness offers relief and a bigger perspective.

And resting in the Witness-Self reinforces the all-important awareness that this is who we truly are — not the overcoats.

Each time we are aware that we are the Witness, not what we are witnessing, awakening occurs.

# 28

# Turn It Over to God

*Letting go gives us freedom,*
*and freedom is the only condition for happiness.*
*If, in our heart, we still cling to anything*
*— anger, anxiety, or possessions —*
*we cannot be free.*

Thich Nhat Hanh

Eventually, each of us will be fully established in our true identity.

We will live each moment knowing who we really are.

Meanwhile, the challenges of the human experience will continue to arise.

Even as we attempt to greet them with love and acceptance and to be with them, we may feel as if we are in over our heads.

At times we feel terrified and overwhelmed.

We may feel lost -- clueless about what to do with what we find.

We may judge ourselves for not knowing how to proceed, but there is a reason we have these feelings and perceptions.

They occur when we come to the edge of our conscious-ness skills and spiritual capacities.

Fortunately, there is an alternative to succumbing to feel-ings of helplessness and hopelessness.

All it asks of us is a shift in viewpoint.

We feel overwhelmed because we can't do it on our own.

We need help.

And we don't need to wait until we can't take it anymore to ask for it.

At any point, we can turn it all over to the Divine.

This is especially helpful when we come upon particularly distressing thoughts and feelings.

We don't need to tough it out on our own.

That doesn't win us any spiritual merit or brownie points.

In fact, believing we have to find our way through the labyrinth of earthly life on our own is a sign that we have forgot-ten an essential truth.

**We are not alone.**

The soul that we are is a drop of divinity that has descend-ed from the vast lake of the Higher Self, which exists on non-physical, higher-dimensional levels.

The Higher Self, in turn, rests within the endless ocean of the Divine, which encompasses All That Is.

The Higher Self overlights the soul's journey through all its lifetimes, and is always available to help us in any way it can.

All we have to do is ask, and that assistance will immedi-ately begin to pour in.

We may also have unseen guides, helpers and teachers, who are always on call.

And many of us were raised to believe that each of us has a Guardian Angel watching over us during our time on Earth.

All of these levels of being act as step-down mechanisms for the immense power, brilliance, and love of the One.

Without these intermediaries, our circuits might be blown.

The Higher Self, for instance, transduces the limitlessness of the Divine, modulating it so that our earthly selves can handle the amplitude.

When we pray to the One, this step-down mechanism is activated, and the Higher Self does its best to ensure that we never receive more divine wattage than we can handle.

Out of the One Great Being, everything in creation emerged.

Ourselves included.

That endless, infinite beingness contains limitless love, intelligence and power.

Since each of us is a part of that divine infinitude, we have direct access to all that it contains.

This is what makes prayer so powerful.

When we enter earthly embodiment, our consciousness focuses nearly exclusively on the outer, tangible aspects of our experience.

This is appropriate, for we have chosen to temporarily operate within the constraints of third-dimensional reality.

But a side effect of this narrow focus is that we forget about the vaster realms from which we came -- the realms in which our invisible helpers live.

Since we no longer remember our higher-dimensional companions, we forget that we can ask them for help.

As we reawaken to the larger reality in which we exist, we rediscover our divine support system.

It includes the beings or levels of consciousness we go to for guidance, loving encouragement, and strength.

In addition to reconnecting with our soul and Higher Self, we may find ourselves communing with a specific divine personage such as Jesus, Quan Yin, or Shiva.

We may also feel an inner resonance with a vaster, more amorphous level of beingness.

We may refer to it as Creator, the Universe, the All in All, or Infinite Intelligence.

It's important to remember that the Divine honors our sovereign free will.

Those who work on behalf of the One do not interfere in our lives.

They only respond to the degree that we have given them the authority to do so.

They listen to our prayers, read what is going on deep in our hearts, and act accordingly.

If, in our heart of hearts, we are truly willing to let go of the steering wheel and turn our challenges over, giving the Divine total authority to do whatever is necessary to resolve the issue, the scope of the inpouring grace is unlimited.

There is never a need to worry about the outcome.

The Divine is infinitely loving, intelligent and powerful.

God sees and knows everything about us and our situation, and only wants what is in the highest and best for us.

The One Great Being and all who work on behalf of That always provide assistance in the gentlest, yet most effective manner possible.

So what is the best way to ask for this divine help and blessing~grace?

An attitude of humility and surrender goes a long way.

We may feel to call to God, our Higher Self, or the soul that we truly are — or all of the above.

We might find ourselves saying something like:

*God, I don't have any idea what to do with all of this. I'm not even sure I can feel everything that is going on within me about it. But since You are Infinite Everything, I know that You will know what needs to happen next. So here, please take it all and do whatever it takes so these feelings can find resolution and I can feel peace.*

It's best to let the words come in your unique way, from your own heart and soul.

The important thing is that the words reflect your willingness to turn it all over -- to stop clutching it all to yourself as if it is *who you are.*

As if this is all that is possible to experience in life.

The option of turning it over is available in every moment.

The following Experience offers a template for how to incorporate this into your awakening process.


## Experience: Turning it Over

Become aware of the breath, your good friend and faithful companion.

As you feel each breath coming in and going back out, ask the wise Self that you are to show your human self something it is time to turn over to the Divine.

It might be an outer challenge, a thought pattern, or a relationship issue.

It could also be a recurring, troubling feeling, or something else that weighs upon your mind and heart.

Whatever it is, invite it to come into your awareness now.

Take a few moments to close your eyes and be with whatever emerges.

Give yourself some empathy for this challenge in yourself or your life.

When you have a clear sense of what is ready to be surrendered to the One, invite your eyes to open and continue reading.

Feel how deeply and truly you want assistance, are willing to turn the issue over, and give the Divine total authority to do whatever is necessary.

With these alignments in consciousness, you open the door to the infinite flow of divine grace.

Now, in your own words, give your challenge to the Divine.

The exact wording isn't important; what matters is your sincere desire to turn the issue over and receive the divine help that is available to you.

Your eyes can be open or closed for this.

It is powerful to speak your intentions aloud, but if that feels awkward or others might hear, focusing on them silently works, too.

As you say the words that come, feel yourself turning it all over.

Notice how that feels.

Do you sense that you have fully given the situation to God?

Or are you hanging on to it in some way?

Sometimes it can be hard to let things go.

They seem to be a part of us.

We might view our issues and challenges as core to who we are.

We may even fear we wouldn't exist without them.

We become attached to whatever we believe is fundamental to our very identity.

If you sense anything like this going on, ask the Divine to remove any identification and attachment to the issue, so you can go free.

You might say something like, "This has nothing to do with who I really am. I don't want to cling to any little bit of this for one more second!"

Then, breathe and feel whatever comes.

Notice how it feels to let go of your hold on this issue or emotion.

Savor the sense of freedom that is replacing what was there within you.

Invite some new words to come to describe your experience, and speak them aloud or to yourself.

You might enjoy journaling about this.

## Reflection:

How do you feel now?

What are you noticing within yourself after turning this situation over to the Divine?

You might be aware of a new inner spaciousness, a quiet mind, or a feeling of emotional well-being and peace.

You may feel a sense of relief as you release the burden of what you have been carrying.

It could be that you sensed an infusion of divine Grace pouring in to help you.

Turning things over to God can become a core part of your life.

The moment you observe yourself compounding the suffering of an issue by clinging to it, you can turn it over.

If a life challenge seems too big and scary to face, you can give it back to the One and ask to be taken on the path through it that is right for you.

Let it go and trust that the journey will unfold at the right time and in the right way.

What a relief to find out we do not need to know what to do with whatever we are experiencing!

All we need to do is be with it and let it go.

Feel what is there, witness it, and release it back into the One.

## Summing Up

This section of the book has presented a simple way to approach whatever might be going on, within and without.

When we notice discomfort of any kind — whether physical, mental, or emotional — we can remind ourselves to **breathe, feel, witness, and turn it over to the Divine**.

Using this simple phrase helps overcoats to peel away, revealing more of the light at our core.

The next section of the book provides step-by-step practice in putting this mantra to use.

Chapter by chapter, we will address each layer of our overcoats.

As we bring awareness to each component and surrender it into the larger Whole, we are bound to feel lighter and brighter.

Overcoats fall away, and the radiance of who we really are shines forth.

Life becomes simpler, happier, and more peaceful.

Isn't that what we all want?

Awakening is experiencing that, in the light of consciousness, our overcoats have no ultimate truth, reality or power.

When we are fully awake, we will experience life without any overcoats at all.

But on the way to fully remembering that we are a divine Self, it helps to be willing to meet what lies within the overcoats.

We can begin by accepting the presence of the disguises we've been wearing over the light at our sacred center.

We can stop making the disguises wrong.

There is nothing bad or shameful about them -- they are simply who we thought we were.

Ultimately, they are illusions.

We are what we are — eternal souls, holy and whole aspects of the One.

As we come to know who we *really* are, we have no need for disguises.

When we see them for what they are, the disguises peel off by themselves.

Once the layers of who we are not receive the love and acceptance they have always wanted, they are as easy to let go of as a Halloween costume once trick-or-treating is over.

# PART FIVE

✢ ✢ ✢

# Taking Off Overcoats

✢ ✢ ✢

# 29

# Become Aware of an Overcoat Removal Opportunity

*In the midst of chaos,*
*there is also opportunity.*

*Sun Tzu*

How do you recognize an opportunity to release overcoats?

At first, you may be aware of a subtle discomfort.

Suddenly, your normal state of equanimity is gone.

Something feels "off."

You might notice or even say, "I don't feel like myself."

Anxiety and agitation may express in bodily symptoms such as a sick feeling in the belly or a tightening in the head.

Emotions may be arising.

The mind may be generating obsessive thoughts and judgments.

It might also be blaming you or others for the apparent problem.

You may feel like hiding or running away.

Or maybe you just want to tell the other person what to do and where to go, using words that were forbidden when you were a child.

In short, you have been triggered by something or someone.

Now that you recognize you are suffering, what will you do next?

Will you see this as a problem, or recognize it as an opportunity?

The mind is probably telling you something is wrong "out there" and needs to be fixed.

The human tendency is to rush into trying to fix the external situation, because that's where the "problem" seems to be.

But the point of power is not in the outer experience, but within ourselves.

Instead of reacting to the storm of thoughts and becoming embroiled within the situation, we can take another path.

We can turn our awareness toward what we are experiencing *inside*.

And we can recognize that, when met with awareness, what is going on  gives us a chance to release overcoats.

The source of our suffering is always the overcoats that are operating just below the surface of our conscious mind.

When we become aware of the inner overcoats that are causing us to react, we can let them go.

Now, the true Self will guide us through the process perfectly.

## Example: Identifying an Opportunity to Let Overcoats Go

Mary returns to work after lunch and sits down at her desk.

She feels centered and at peace, happy to launch into her next project.

Mary likes her job; it offers her a wealth of creative opportunities, and she's good at what she does.

She picks up her work cell phone and notices a short text from her boss, who is out of the office today.

He wants to meet with her tomorrow morning at 9.

The calmness Mary had been feeling is suddenly punctuated by a roiling in her stomach.

Her throat clenches.

*What is this about?* she wonders.

Her mind starts to race.

Mary's overcoats have been activated, and she is identifying with them.

Old patterns of fear and self-doubt rise to the surface.

*I thought the presentation yesterday went well.*

*The new clients seemed to like it.*

*But maybe I was imagining that.*

Now, a very old overcoat adds its chronic worry to the mix.

*I poured so much into that presentation.*

*What did I do wrong?*

Mary is now in the experience of suffering.

The peace and centeredness of her true Self are shrouded by layers of overcoats.

Somehow, Mary makes it through the rest of the day.

On the way home, she suddenly becomes aware that this situation is a doorway, an opportunity to get free.

It's a chance to bring consciousness to what's going on. Mary realizes she is not a victim of the situation.

When she reaches her apartment, she makes a cup of tea and sits in her favorite chair.

She is now ready to investigate the situation with her awareness.

In the following chapter, Mary's story continues through the next steps in the process of releasing overcoats.

Are you ready to embark on your own journey into over-coat-free living?

The next Experience begins the process.

In this and succeeding chapters, you will practice what you have been reading and learning about overcoat removal.

Each step in the process builds naturally upon the previous segments.

Let each part of the process take as long as it wants to take.

There is no rush here.


## Experience: Identifying an Overcoat Removal Opportunity

To begin, set aside some time to go within.

Invite your body to get comfortable, and make sure you will not be interrupted.

Start by letting your awareness rest on your breathing, feeling each breath come in and go back out.

Breath by breath, feel your consciousness shifting from the outer world to your inner realms.

Ask to be made aware of an issue or challenge you would like to investigate.

It may be a recent situation, or an ongoing theme in your life.

This is not about searching with your mind.

Instead, invite your true Self to bring it to your attention in an unmistakable way.

When you feel clear about what it is, simply be with it for a few moments.

Then, briefly describe it in your notebook or journal.

As you consider this challenge, you might find yourself becoming aware of some of the bodily sensations and emotions around the issue.

You may notice thoughts and judgments about it, too.

Your mind may contain mental images related to the situation.

You are beginning to become aware of some of the overcoats you are wearing.

We are going to embark on a journey through the layers of overcoats that have accumulated in connection with this challenge.

In "real life" the layers are usually mixed together in a stew of thoughts and feelings and memories.

For the purposes of this practice session, though, we will address one layer at a time.

This is helpful in learning how to identify the various types of overcoat layers we are wearing.

It also helps us to not feel as overwhelmed by what is going on.

Addressing one layer at a time, rather than trying to deal with the entire jumbled situation, feels reassuringly doable.

Layer by layer, we will bring awareness, acceptance, and love to whatever we come upon.

We will breathe, feel, witness, and turn it all over to God.

In this way, it is possible to simply and easily step out of the overcoats and into the freedom that is our birthright.

Not some distant day, but right now.

# 30

# Breathe, Feel, Witness, and Turn it Over to the Divine

*The past, present, and future mingle*
*and pull us backward, forward, or fix us in the present.*
*We are made up of layers, cells, constellations.*

*Anais Nin*

Now it is time for the next step in the overcoat removal process.

It is actually a series of steps, and the following chapters will focus on one at a time.

Any time we are not feeling the peace and harmony of our true Self, we are experiencing our overcoats.

Once we have realized we are at the threshold of an opportunity to get free, it is time to use the simple mantra presented in Part Four of this book.

It goes like this: *Breathe, feel, witness, and turn it over to the Divine.*

If we try to do this all at once, we will feel overwhelmed.

So we'll break it down into its components and focus on one at a time.

## Example: Breathe, Feel, Witness, and Turn it Over to God

As she settles into her comfortable chair, Mary, whom we met in the previous chapter, lets her eyes close and becomes aware of her breathing.

She remembers she doesn't need to make the breath be a certain way; she can simply let herself be breathed.

Breath by breath, Mary feels herself relaxing.

As a few breaths come and go, Mary feels more centered in who she really is.

Her awareness has returned to her Self.

It is no longer focused externally.

Centered in the soul that she is, Mary feels ready to contemplate the text from her boss.

Now, Mary notices the sick feeling in her belly returning.

She also becomes aware of some mild heart palpitations, and feels fear.

Her mind begins to churn out a litany of suffering.

*What if I lose my job?*

*It'd be hard to find one I like as much.*

*And it could take a while.*

*How will I make the house payments?*

Mary continues to inwardly invite anything else to come forth.

More fears arise.

More thoughts clamor for attention.

She hears judgments of herself in some of the thoughts.

*Did I miss something important in my presentation?*

*Maybe I didn't spend enough time on it.*

*Maybe I am just not capable of doing this job after all.*

As she witnesses it all coming and going, Mary reminds herself to come back to her breathing and let her awareness rest there.

Then she remembers she can turn it all over to God.

*What a relief!*

*I don't have to know what to do with any of it!*

She imagines gathering the entire situation into a bundle and then gives it all to the Divine.

It was never really hers, anyway, she realizes.

It only seemed to be her "problem."

Mary sits in silence as she feels herself resting in the One.

She asks if there is anything she can see or know about the situation, and quietly waits to see if anything comes in.

*This is my old pattern,* she realizes.

*If anything even slightly threatening happens, I go right into fear and doubt.*

*There is really no reason to assume that my boss is upset with me.*

*That's just where my mind tends to go.*

Mary sits with this insight, absorbing it.

A feeling of peace begins to come in.

Her body is releasing some of its tension and discomfort, and she feels more relaxed about the situation.

*It will be what it will be*, she realizes.

*And God will be with me, no matter what.*

She feels lighter now, and realizes her stomach is grumbling.

Time to make some dinner.

*Maybe I'll watch a movie*, she thinks.

*That sounds like fun.*

When the next morning arrives, Mary dresses with a bit of extra care for her meeting with her boss.

She isn't consumed with fear, as she had been the day before, but she can feel remnants of doubt lurking around the edges of her calmness.

She turns the fear and doubt over to the Divine and asks for strength and courage to face whatever the meeting brings.

Driving to work, she feel herself held within divine arms and knows all will be well, no matter what unfolds.

At 9:00, her boss welcomes her into his office and invites Mary to take a seat.

"I just wanted to tell you that the new clients *really* liked your presentation," he says warmly, "and have decided to go with us for their next campaign."

"Well done!" he adds with a smile.

"If all goes as we think it will, there's a raise in your future," he finishes.

Mary is far more pleased than her expression reveals.

Her job is not only secure, she is also in line for a salary increase.

And only she knows how this incident has served her evolution as a soul.

There is no guarantee that all of our life issues will resolve as easily and positively as Mary's did.

You may need to revisit your issue many times before it feels resolved.

Like any skill, the more you apply what you have learned, the easier it will become.

Give yourself empathy.

Learning any new skill presents challenges.

You are creating new neural grooves each time you use this process when a challenge arises.

It can never hurt to bring awareness to our inner world, and the benefits remain with us, no matter what happens in the outer situation.

Every bit of self-awareness we cultivate is actually Self-awareness, for as we become aware of what lies within our overcoats, they de-densify and dissolve, revealing the radiance of the true Self ever more fully.

In the following chapters, you will be putting into practice the principles and steps discussed above.

No matter how it goes, you will emerge from each chapter's Experience with greater awareness of your own inner landscape.

This is the sacred territory that reveals itself as we breathe, feel, witness, and turn whatever we find over to the Divine.

This is how we find our way Home to the true, divine Self that we are.

# 31

# Drop into the Breath

*You practice and you get better.*
*It's really very simple.*

*Philip Glass*

Cultivating the ability to drop into the breath at any moment expedites the process of awakening.

Resting in the breath helps us to meet whatever is happening, within and without, with a welcoming attitude.

We are inviting it to reveal itself to us.

There is no push or shove in this — just a gentle beckoning to whatever is there, waiting for us to meet it with love and acceptance.

As we rest in the breath, we become aware that we are being breathed.

We are not making our breathing happen.

This is just as true of every other aspect of the process of releasing overcoats.

We are making ourselves available for whatever is ready to occur, but we are not "doing" anything.

Each breath helps us to open to the mystery of what is to follow.

## Example: Being with the Breath

Here is an excerpt from the story about Mary in the previous chapter.

*As she settles into her comfortable chair, Mary lets her eyes close and becomes aware of her breathing.*

*She remembers she doesn't need to make the breath be a certain way; she can simply let herself be breathed.*

*Breath by breath, Mary feels herself relaxing.*

*As a few breaths come and go, Mary feels more centered in who she really is.*

*Her awareness has returned to her Self.*

*It is no longer focused externally.*

*Centered in the Self that she is, Mary feels ready to contemplate the text from her boss and all that it brought up for her.*

Notice the way that dropping into her breath helped Mary to relax.

The simple choice to focus on her breathing gave Mary an anchor-point.

Resting in that safe space, Mary then felt ready to investigate the other layers of her experience.

## Experience: Being with the Breath

Now it is your turn.

Find a comfortable position that will support you in opening to the breath.

Make sure you will not be interrupted, and take a few moments to settle in.

As you consider the situation you are going to investigate, become aware of your breathing.

Feel the breath coming in through your nostrils and then going back out.

Simply feel the breath doing what breath does.

No need to make anything happen.

Just feel and witness each breath.

Feel your awareness shifting from the outer situation to your inner world.

At its core is the realm of the Self.

As you feel the breath taking you deeper into your inner world, remember the Self is who you really are.

It knows how to guide you through every challenge that arises.

Sink into this truth.

There is the Self, and there are the overcoats that are layered over your innermost being.

Continue to feel the breath breathing you.

Notice how it feels to be more deeply rooted in your true nature.

Now, consider the issue you are exploring.

If it involves a painful memory, remember what it was like as though it is happening right now.

As you feel the breath coming and going, continue to re-live this experience.

And be with whatever is present in you about it right now.

If your challenge is a situation or dilemma you currently face, simply be with whatever arises about it.

You are giving yourself the gift of being with all that is going on within you.

All you need to do is be with it.

Feel the breath breathing you while you are present with whatever you are experiencing.

It's as simple as that.

When this feels complete for now, you might like to journal about your experience.

Then rest for a bit and drink some cool water before you go on to the next chapter.

# 32

# Bodily Sensations

*Looking at our difficulties*
*as if they were enemies*
*is the lid which keeps them in place.*

Stephen Schwartz
*The Compassionate Presence*


The breath is your anchor, the lifeline you can hang on to in a mental or emotional storm.

Focusing on the breath gives your awareness a peaceful place to rest, no matter what may be going on within you or around you.

Once you have connected with the breath, you are ready to turn your awareness toward the bodily sensations that are present in relation to your challenging issue.

To see how this works, let's return to Mary's story.


## Example: Being with Bodily Sensations

As Mary drops into her breath and begins to explore her inner world, she becomes aware of some clear and definite body-sensations.

*Now, Mary notices the sick feeling in her belly returning.*

*She also notices some mild heart palpitations.*

Your own bodily sensations may be clear-cut like Mary's, or more vague and diffuse.

They may be localized, or spread throughout your physical body.

Whatever you notice, simply be with it and feel what is present.

The next Experience will guide you through the steps of the "mantra": *Breathe, feel, witness, and turn it over to God.*

## Experience: Being with Bodily Sensations

PART ONE: Breathe and Feel Bodily Sensations

To access this layer, read the statement in your journal describing the issue.

Then, close your eyes and become aware of your breathing.

Allow the breath to carry your awareness within.

Now, as you sit with the issue, invite any and all body-sensations connected to it to arise.

Begin with the one that surfaces first, or the one that is the strongest.

Feel whatever is present.

Ir might be a tightness, or a dull ache, or a sharp pain, or another sensation somewhere in your physical body.

Feel it and breathe into it.

Let it be the way it is.

As one sensation receives the attention it has been wanting, it may give way to another.

Follow the trail of sensations wherever it takes you.

A pain in your belly may subside, only to be replaced by a throbbing in your temples.

A sensation may also intensify before it gives way to the next.

Whatever unfolds, all you need to do is follow the trail of energy as it unspools.

This is how the overcoats of bodily discomfort unravel and fall away.

Let this part of the process take as long as it wants.

When the sensations become quiet, or you feel you have been with them as much as you can, it is time for the next step in the process.

PART TWO: Witness Bodily Sensations

Once again, become aware of the Self that you are, beneath all the layers of overcoats on the surface of your being.

Now, *witness* the bodily sensations you have just experienced through the eyes of the true Self.

Some may still be present.

You can also observe what *was* there.

See the sensations; witness them.

They are what they are, and you do not need to know what to do with any of them.

Just remember that ultimately, they have no truth, no reality, no power.

Even the strongest and most disturbing bodily sensations are only illusory apparitions passing through the vastness of the Self that you are.

You, as a divine soul, are simply *in the experience of* whatever is going on within you.

As a divine Self, you can remind your human self: *These sensations have no ultimate truth, power, or reality.*

Simply be with them and witness them as the soul that you are.

At some point, being with the bodily sensations connected to your issue or challenge will feel complete for now.

It is time to turn them over to the Divine.

PART THREE: Turn Bodily Sensations Over to God

Are you ready to turn over any body-sensations that are still present?

With the simple innocence of a little child, talk to the Divine.

You might say something like this: "God, I know these sensations are not who I really am. Please take them from me so that I can go free."

Feel your willingness to release them all, and let them go.

Feel the Infinite Oneness taking them into Itself as you let go of them.

All of the sensations will be transmuted back into pure life energy in the right timing.

It may happen right away, or take some time.

Feel the lightness and spaciousness in the spaces where those sensations once lived in you.

Enjoy the newfound sense of openness where discomfort used to be.

You are releasing overcoats of bodily unease, tightness, and contraction.

Layer by layer, you are finding your way through the challenge you are exploring.

# 33

# Emotions

*I don't believe that life is supposed to make you feel good,*
*or to make you feel miserable either.*
*Life is just supposed to make you feel.*

Gloria Naylor

During the previous chapter's Experience, you might have noticed that alongside the physical sensations were emotions such as grief or anger.

These comprise the next layer of overcoats we encounter when we turn our awareness within.

Our fear of our feelings is often the first hurdle we encounter as our awareness moves toward them.

The first step is to acknowledge that fear of feeling is present.

Some trepidation is normal in the face of doing something new.

But an overwhelming amount of fear may indicate that you need additional time or support to move toward your feelings.

In that case, read this chapter, if you like, but do not attempt the Experience until you feel ready.

Love yourself and know that your divine Self will bring the feelings you are ready to face to your attention as you are ready to feel them.

If this feels overwhelming, consider seeking out professional assistance.

Working with a skilled facilitator provides a sturdy container for the feelings that seem too threatening to face alone.

## Example: Being Fully Present with Feelings

When Mary received the text from her boss asking her to meet with him the next morning, the feeling she recognized was *fear*.

The chapter after this one is all about this powerful emotion.

As Mary read the text message from her boss, many other feelings may also have been present.

Mary may have felt *overwhelmed, nervous,* and *worried.*

She may also have felt *troubled, anxious, uncomfortable, alarmed, uneasy, distressed,* and even *panicky.*

Mary definitely seemed *upset.*

She was also *concerned* about her job security.

In any challenging situation, it is likely that a host of feelings are present.

As we get in touch with one emotion and feel it, that feeling typically leads us to another.

For instance, the hot fire of surface anger may give way to underlying sadness and disappointment.

Ultimately, we may encounter an all-too-familiar, deep-down feeling of hopelessness.

As you work with the following Experience, allow the feelings to surface in their own way.

This will probably have little or nothing to do with the way "logic" or "reason" think the process ought to be going.

## Experience: Being Fully Present with Feelings

To begin, find a comfortable position for your body, one it can maintain for a while.

As in previous Experiences, you can alternate reading a few lines and going within to experience them.

Or, read these directions now, and refer back to them during the Experience as needed.

Let your eyes close; feel and witness the breath moving in and out.

Feel your awareness returning to your inner landscape.

Again become aware of the challenging situation you are exploring.

PART ONE: Breathe, Feel, and Witness Emotions

Once again, drop into experiencing the breath breathing you.

Allow a few breaths to come and go as your awareness settles into your inner world.

You might feel sensations related to the breath, as well as other sensations in various places in your body.

As you become aware of a sensation somewhere in your body, breathe into it and feel what is there.

Then ask if there is an emotion within the sensation that is ready to be met and felt.

As the feeling emerges into your awareness, invite the breath into it and feel what is present.

Simply breathe and feel.

No need to do anything with what is arising -- just feel it.

It is what it is.

When there is no resistance to a feeling, as it is allowed and felt, it releases.

You may sense it losing energy and dissolving.

Sometimes, as we meet a feeling, it grows stronger, especially if it has been waiting for some time to be acknowledged and felt.

If this occurs, continue to be aware of the breath and invite your awareness to move toward the intensity of the feeling.

Breathe and feel, moving from the periphery toward the center of the feeling sensations.

Some feelings, especially deep, old ones, may not move through right away.

If a feeling seems overwhelming, step back and observe the emotion from a safe distance.

In time, the energetic charge of the feeling may subside, allowing you to drop into feeling the emotion.

The feeling may also need more acceptance and compassion from you.

Whatever the emotion, you can meet it with empathy and caring.

As you continue to be present to your emotions, you may find that feeling them blends with witnessing them.

Witnessing helps us to stand back from the emotions.

When we can observe them, we are not swept up in them.

Now, we can see them through the eyes of the Self.

This helps us to remember that these feelings are not who we are.

Let witnessing and feeling begin to merge.

You are feeling what is present, and also observing it.

PART TWO: Turn Emotions Over to the Divine

When feeling and observing the emotions feels complete for now, gather up all of the feelings that have surfaced.

Feel your willingness to release the burden of these emotions.

Now, turn them over to the One.

Ask the Divine to completely dissolve this layer of your overcoats connected to the issue you are exploring, in the perfect way and timing.

You've done what you could do; now it is time for divine grace.

Give it all up as a little child might, with simplicity and innocence.

You might say, "I don't know what to do with any of this, God, but You do. So here — take it all, please."

Release it into the Divine and know that it is being embraced within the totality of Life itself.


## Reflection:

Feelings are often the most powerful layer of an issue or challenge.

At first, they can feel heavy and immovable.

But the simple act of being with feelings helps the overcoat layers to decompress.

Breathing space into the layers, along with feeling and witnessing them,  allows emotions to move through rather than continue to accumulate.

Turning it all over to the One invites grace to pour into the situation.

The newfound spaciousness within us can be a revelation.

We begin to discover the free and open way we were meant to experience life.

We're getting a taste of what life without overcoats is like.

# 34

# Fears

*The best way out is always through.*

*Robert Frost*

As we feel our way through the layers of feeling, we eventually get down to the fears at the bottom of the pile.

When these fears remain unconscious and unexamined, they prolong the presence of the issue in our lives.
34
Conversely, as we bring awareness to the fears, they can be recognized and felt.

Now they are no longer buried in the unconscious.

Like all other feelings, they can move through us rather than continue to be stored deep within.

This helps the issue itself to resolve and release.

As overcoats of fear fall away, we feel lighter and freer, ready to experience life in new ways.

## Example: Being with Fears

When Mary read the message from her boss, the emotion of fear arose.

A generalized sensation of fear was accompanied by fears with particular associations.

Mary probably felt fear of the boss's displeasure.

She might have feared that her work was not good enough.

Ultimately, Mary feared losing her job.

## Experience: Being with Fears

After reading these brief directions, allow your eyes to close.

Once again, invite the issue you are investigating to be present in your awareness.

PART ONE: Breathe, Feel, and Witness Fear

As you become aware of your breathing, ask to be shown any fears connected to this situation.

Allow a few moments for them to come into your consciousness.

Write each fear down in your notebook.

Now, allow yourself to feel each fear in turn.

Breathe into it and invite it to reveal itself to you.

If *feeling* the fear is too overwhelming or scary, *witness* it.

See it for what it is.

The fear will probably try to convince you that it is the truth about the situation.

But it is merely a fear.

Like all other layers of overcoats, it has no ultimate truth, reality, or power.

Since fear is usually expressed in bodily contraction, breathing into it helps  the contraction to release.

As this happens, you may feel your energy spreading out and taking up more space within your body.

You might also feel the fear beginning to let go and and move through.

Continue to invite the fear to reveal deeper layers of itself to you.

Notice the transformative power of bringing awareness into the fears rather than allowing them to persist unquestioned.

Feel the difference in your inner experience from breathing into, feeling, and witnessing the fear.

This is how it feels as overcoats fall away.

PART TWO: Turn the Fears Over to God

Now, gather up all the fears that are or were present and give them to the One Who Knows what to do with them.

Admit that you do not have a clue about how to deal with them, and ask for help from the Divine.

Notice if any part of you is hanging on to the fears, believing they are real.

Continue to turn the fears over as you become aware of them.

Let the process take as long as it takes.

Observe how you feel once it seems to be complete for now.

What is your experience of yourself?

## Reflection:

What was it like to allow fear to be present rather than turn away from it?

How does your issue appear now, after turning over your feelings and fears to the Divine?

How do you feel after this Experience?

# 35

# The Contents of the Mind

*It often happens that I wake at night
and begin to think about a pressing problem
and decide I must tell the Pope about it.
Then I wake up completely and remember
that I am the Pope.*

*Pope John XXIII*

As Chapter Twenty discussed, our feelings and fears are based on what is going on in the mind.

When we bring awareness to the mind, we will uncover at least one idea or belief that seems to justify every feeling or fear we have.

This mind-stuff is the "reason" we feel or fear what we do.

It is important to remind ourselves that not one of these "reasons" is real or true.

Each one is an *idea* about reality — not the way reality actually is.

## Example: Feelings, Fears, and Their Associated Beliefs

As Mary got in touch with her fear, a host of mind-stuff poured out.

*What if I lose my job?*

*It'd be hard to find one I like as much.*

*And it could take a while.*

*How will I pay my mortgage?*

These thoughts seemed to give Mary "reasons" to feel afraid.

Beliefs can hide in fearful questions like the ones Mary found herself asking.

*What if I lose my job?* contains the belief that she could lose her job.

*How will I pay the mortgage?* includes the possibility that Mary will run out of money.

Mary's mind might even be assuming that she **will** lose her job and have no money.

The mind usually looks at any fearful possibility and treats it as a fact.

This chain of thought goes something like, *I am afraid __ will happen. Therefore, it WILL happen.*

With this kind of assumptive thinking likely to be going on, no wonder so few of us are willing to examine our fears!

When we are upset, the contents of the mind often fly by in a stream of consciousness — or, more accurately, unconsciousness.

In our troubled state, it is tempting to believe what the mind is saying.

When we can witness what is passing by, we detach from it.

Now, we are less likely to take the bait and believe what the mind insists is real.

Ultimately, we remember that not one thing the fearful mind says is true.

That is why it is extremely helpful, whenever we notice a belief, to ask ourselves, "Do I know for sure that this is true?"

This helps the mind to release its subconscious assumption that the thought is true.

We feel afraid, or disappointed, or whatever emotion is arising, because we believe the idea behind it is true.

We unglue our attachment to the thought when we realize it has no truth, reality, or power.

In the process, we also release our attachment to the feelings that are causing us to suffer.

When Mary examined her fears, the main one was *I'm afraid I will lose my job.*

The belief driving Mary's fear is *I am going to lose my job.*

If Mary believes the idea that she will lose her job, no wonder she feels afraid!

But it is only an idea, and has no more reality or truth than anything else the mind generates.

It helps to remember that believing what the mind comes up with is optional, and not recommended.

## Experience: Looking at the Beliefs Behind Feelings and Fears

For this Experience, you will need a pen and your journal or a pad of paper. Set them nearby.

Allow your body to come into a comfortable position and invite your eyes to close.

Become aware of your breathing, and witness~feel a few breaths as they come and go.

Feel your awareness shifting to your inner world of sensations, feelings and thoughts.

Now, ask to be made aware of a feeling or fear related to your life issue or challenge.

Feel whatever is present within you.

Ask the feeling or fear to tell you about itself.

This will begin to flush out the ideas behind the emotions.

If fear is present, ask, *What bad thing is going to happen if this fear is true?*

Proceed in this way through all of the feelings and fears you have uncovered.

When you have a clear sense of the ideas that lie behind the feelings and fears, let your eyes open.

On a page of your journal or a sheet of paper, create two columns.

In the first column, write down each feeling or fear.

Use the format *I feel*_____.

Then, ask to be shown the beliefs that drive the feeling or fear.

Each of your feelings or fears will have a corresponding "reason" or "justification."

Write this in the second column next to the feeling or fear in column one.

After listing all the ideas that surface, survey them all.

Remember, they are just ideas.

Has buying into these thoughts brought suffering?

Now, examine each one and ask, *Do I know that this is true?*

Ask to be shown all you can see about each belief.

Continue on until each thought has been addressed.

Then turn them all over to the One and ask that these and all other ideas about the situation be absorbed within Infinite Intelligence.

You might also affirm something like, *May only the truth remain within me!*

## Reflection:

What did you find as you uncovered the beliefs behind the feelings and fears?

Were you able to say that any of the beliefs is absolutely true?

How do the feelings and fears look now?

What do you take away from this experience?

## Other Mind-Stuff

In addition to the beliefs that drive our feelings and fears, many other ideas and concepts may be present in a given situation.

Some of them may be judgments, which the next chapter focuses on.

The following Experience provides an opportunity to invite any other contents of the mind connected with the situation you are exploring to come to light.

As you witness and detach from these ideas and beliefs, they lose their power to control how the situation unfolds.

The overcoats of mind fall away, and the truth of the Self is revealed.

## Experience: Witnessing Additional Mind-Stuff

Place your journal or notebook nearby, and alternate reading a few lines of the following directions with closing your eyes and going within.

Invite your awareness to rest on your breathing.

Feel each breath coming and going, and drop into your inner world.

Briefly review the layers of overcoats you have already investigated.

You have brought consciousness into the bodily sensations associated with the issue you are exploring, as well as the emotions and fears and their underlying beliefs.

Now, invite any other mental content to be present in your awareness.

It may include beliefs about the situation, concepts about what is possible, or theories about why it is the way it is.

Whatever you notice, write it down.

You may notice a part of the mind wanting to believe what you have written.

Some of the ideas may seem very real and true.

But are they?

Witness each idea you have written down through the eyes of the Self.

Ask the Self to reveal the truth about each idea you have written down.

You may want to write down these new revelations, too.

Allow plenty of time for this process.

When it feels complete, turn it all over to the Infinite Intelligence that can reveal even more about these concepts and interpretations.

Invite that endless wisdom to pour into your mind and replace illusions with truth.

Allow as much time for this as it wants.

When the infusion feels complete, ask yourself this simple question:

How do those ideas look now?


## Reflection:

As we investigate a challenging situation, its layers do not all peel away at once.

Deeper layers of feelings, fears, and their associated thoughts may continue to surface over time until the situation is fully resolved.

When they do, use this process again.

Drop into your breathing, feel the body sensations and emotions, and identify the thoughts that lie behind the feelings and fears.

Invite any other mental content to reveal itself.

In this way, you will uncover more beliefs.

Then you can ask if they are true.

Turn them over to the divine Self that you are and ask Infinite Intelligence to dispel the veils of illusion that have clouded the mind.

And give thanks for the liberation that lies on the other side of believing these limiting concepts.

# 36

# Judgments

*The more one judges,*
*the less one loves.*

*Honore de Balzac*

As you became aware of the thoughts connected with your life issue during the previous chapter's Experience, you probably noticed that some of them were actually judgments.

In any challenging situation, judgments of ourselves, others, or the circumstances themselves are often present.

Any time we hear the mind insisting something or someone should be different, we are in the presence of a judgment.

The words **should** and **ought** are sure signs judgment is going on.

Do you hear the judgment in each of the following sentences?

*He should take better care of his dog.*

*They ought to clean up their yard.*

We may judge the behavior of others, as in these examples, and have definite ideas about how they ought to be acting.

On a deeper level, we may judge the people themselves.

We pass judgment on people when we "call them names" that denigrate their very being.

Forms of the verb **to be** indicate the presence of such condemning judgments.

These judgments often begin with *He/she/they are* _____, as in:

*She's a slut.*

*He is a worthless idiot.*

Although positive judgments of someone's very being are much less frequent in human speech, they do exist.

As with negative judgments, those who make such pronouncements put themselves in the position of One On High, believing they are entitled to judge.

Consider these common examples of positive judgments.

*You're an angel.*

*He's a pillar of our community.*

*She's a great person.*

And how often do we tell our beloved pet, *"Good dog"*?

## Example: Being with Judgments

As Mary examined the contents of her mind, she noticed some judgments among the thoughts that surfaced.

*Maybe I just didn't spend enough time on [my presentation].*

This implies a belief that Mary **should** have spent more time on it.

*Maybe I am just not capable of doing this job after all.*

Here, she is questioning not only the quality of her presentation, but also her overall ability to do the job.

These judgments are about her performance.

They may have deep roots, reflecting a lifetime of self-doubt.

Hidden beneath the surface concerns may be a much deeper judgment about her very being: *I am a failure.*

How many of us harbor this deep-down judgment?

We may go through life feeling pretty good about ourselves, but when trouble arises, the mind reverts to this condemning thought about ourselves.

We often adopt positive judgments in an attempt to balance out or replace these bottom-line self-judgments.

*I'm awesome!*

*We rule!*

But paving over the deeper, more troubling contents of the mind with better ones never really works.

This makes as much sense as slathering frosting over a festering compost bucket, in hopes the smell of rotten food will go away.

Far better to identify the destructive overcoats of judgment, and watch our newfound awareness erode their solidity.

As overcoats of self-hating judgment fall away, we are more able to see ourselves and one another through the eyes of the soul, which never judges.

Then, we have no need to puff ourselves up with affirmations of grandeur.

We simply see our radiant magnificence, and live as That.

✤ ✤ ✤

The following Experience has three parts.

Each is designed to increase your awareness of how judgment looks and feels.

As the mechanics of judgment are revealed, the scratchy, uncomfortable overcoats of judgment automatically begin to fall away.

## Experience: Being with Judgments

PART ONE: Judgments about Yourself

Find a comfortable position for your physical body, and place your notebook or journal nearby.

After reading these directions, invite your eyes to close.

Let your awareness rest on the breath.

Feel your energy settling in and your awareness turning inward.

Now, become aware of the situation you are exploring.

Ask to be shown the judgments of yourself that are a part of this challenge.

Question yourself: How should I be "more," "better," or "different"?

In your journal or notebook, begin with "I should" and fill in the blank.

Write whatever pops into the mind first, without thinking about it.

*I should* _____.

*I should* _____.

When judgments arise insisting that we should act or be other than we are, messages of condemnation may lurk right behind them.

Inner voices of judgment may condemn your very being-ness.

These statements often begin with *I am.*

For instance, *I am a failure.*

See if any of these mega-judgments are present.

In your journal or notebook, complete the sentence: *I am*
_____.

Many responses may arise. Write them all down.

Continue writing until there is a natural pause in the flow of judgments.

Now, reread what you have written.

Are you surprised by what has emerged?

Dismayed?

Ashamed?

Or are these familiar thoughts you have heard a thousand times before?

PART TWO: Are the Judgments True?

Go back to the first "I should" statement you wrote down.

Read it aloud.

Ask yourself, "Is this true?"

Can you or anybody say for sure this is what you should be doing or being in this situation?

Breathe open some space in which the judgment can simply be what it is -- an idea about how you ought to be or act.

*Witness* the power of this negative statement about your-self.

Then *feel* what it has been like to live beneath the burden of this belief.

Have the feelings associated with buying into this judgment made the issue harder to resolve?

Does this judgments lead to other self-judgments or self-condemnation?

You may recognize a negative feedback loop here -- a Mobius strip of suffering begetting more suffering.

It's helpful to remind ourselves that no judgment has any truth, reality, or power.

Is it time to turn the judgment over to God and ask for help to go beyond it?

You might say something like, "God, I feel so tired of being weighed down by this endless cycle of judgment. Please lift it from me so I can experience life without it."

Breathe and feel what it is like to turn the judgment over to the One.

Notice if any part of you still believes the judgment is true.

Turn that over, too.

See if you can feel the judgment lifting off, like a balloon freed of its ballast.

Enjoy a deep breath in your new, lightened-up state.

On the exhale, let go of any remaining residues of judgment.

Now, let yourself fully experience what this situation or challenge would be  like without this overcoat of judgment weighing you down.

This is more than a mental exercise -- really *feel* what it is like to be free of this restricting idea about yourself.

When you let yourself fully experience this freedom, you'll want it to last.

That means you'll be less likely to agree with the next judgmental idea the mind comes up with.

It's futile to wish that the mind would stop doing this, because, as you will recall, the mind's function is to generate thoughts.

But *believing* them is optional -- and only leads to suffering.

If no one gives any energy to a toddler throwing a tantrum, the kicking, screaming frenzy soon stops.

Similarly, when we no longer feed the mind by giving power to the thoughts it generates, it tends to quiet down.

Repeat this process with each of the judgments of yourself you have listed on paper.

This may take some time.

It might make sense to examine a few judgments each day.

You can also continue to add more judgments as you discover them.

This is how we bring awareness to the judgmental contents of the mind.

Once they are seen in the light of consciousness, these overcoats never have the same power over us.

PART THREE: Judgments of Others

In the previous parts of this Experience, you brought awareness to the mind's judgments of yourself.

Now, you can investigate the mind's judgments of any others who are involved in the challenging situation.

You might begin with the judgments of their behavior.

A simple form to use is, *He/she/they should* _____.

Begin with one person's name and complete the sentence.

Do this for the first person until the mind goes quiet.

Then begin again with a new person's name.

Pause when you have listed all the judgments of everyone's behavior.

Now, check for the deeper, more severe judgments that condemn someone's beingness, not just their actions.

To flush these out, begin with *He/she is* _____, or *They are* _____.

You may feel ashamed or embarrassed as these denigrating statements come forth, but don't let that stop you.

Get them all out.

These overcoats are burdening you, and they are certainly not helping the situation to resolve.

When your list feels complete for now, use the same process of investigation as before with each one.

Go back to the first judgment you wrote down.

Read it aloud, and ask yourself, *Is it true?*

*Can you or anybody say for sure this is what that person should be doing or being?*

Allow a few breaths to open up some space in which the judgment can simply be what it is -- an idea about how someone else ought to be or act.

Feel what it has been like to see this person through the eyes of this belief.

How has this affected the way you relate to the person?

Do you want to continue to buy into this judgment?

What might happen if you let it go?

Write down what you are discovering.

At some point, it may occur to you that the mind has been holding some of its judgments of others for a very long time, and that those judgments are as unkind and unfair as the ones about yourself.

When it is time to turn them all over to the Divine, let that unfold just as you did with the judgments of yourself.

You might say something like, "God, I really don't want to go on judging _____ (insert names). I see how unloving and unfair that is. Please help me to see these beings through your eyes — the eyes of my soul. Please lift all of these judgments from my mind and replace them with the way my true Self sees these beings."

You may also want to ask for forgiveness for all the judgments the mind has held as true, both about yourself and about others.

## Reflection:

What are you discovering about the judgments that have been unconsciously running in your mind?

What was it like to turn them over to the Divine?

Did a part of the mind want to hang on to any of the judgments, believing it was justified in doing so?

Remember, there is no need to try to talk that part out of its position.

Just observe it and listen to its views.

Then notice what judging does to your own energy and awareness.

How do you feel when you cling to judgments of yourself?

What is your life like when you believe your judgments of others are true?

## The Overcoats of Judgment

We might summarize the mechanism of judgment with a simple schematic.

There is what is going on, within and without.

And then there are the judgments about what is going on.

Judgment never arises from the true Self.

It is always an expression of our overcoats.

And when we judge, we are not perceiving the Self of anyone else, but only *their* overcoats.

The same is true when we judge ourselves.

We are not seeing the Self, only our overcoats.

Thoughts that "I should be different" and "They (or the situation) should be different" pile on the overcoats faster than just about any other beliefs.

And the even more damaging judgments -- those that assess the very beingness of ourselves or others -- form some of the heaviest overcoats of all.

They ascribe qualities and characteristics that have nothing to do with anyone's true nature.

These hate-filled judgments diminish their very being — and our own.

When we believe these thoughts, the truth of the Self is veiled beneath overcoats of harsh judgments.

We are no longer seeing ourselves, others, or life itself through the loving eyes of the Self.

Our judgments reflect the belief that overcoats are real.

Not only that, judging indicates that we believe we *are* our overcoats, and they are theirs.

Now we are really lost.

Each time we believe judging thoughts, the layers of our own overcoats compact and grow weightier.

Judgments shut down the free and natural flow of our life-force.

They stifle our energy beneath a blanket of hateful thoughts.

When we believe them and repeat them aloud, they close our heart and mind.

This can only diminish our awareness that we are the radiant, divine Self.

Each judgment we hang on to, whether it is about ourselves or others, does a little more damage to our biochemical and energetic makeup.

If we go on judging, our mental, emotional and physical health is likely to suffer.

The luminosity, clarity, and love of the Self become buried beneath overcoats of condemnation.

No wonder we feel resentful, frustrated, and stuck, living beneath layer upon layer of making ourselves, others, and life itself wrong, wrong, wrong.

## The Hubris of Judging

Judging ourselves and one another presumes we know more than God about how we or they should be.

When we judge, we are directly denying the truth of who we, and they, really are.

We are literally cursing ourselves or others.

Doesn't that seem just the slightest bit absurd, not to mention cruel?

If there were a better way for you to be, or a better way for your life to be going, wouldn't that be happening?

And wouldn't that be just as true for others?

We will all continue to evolve and awaken, of course.

But that happens most easily when we accept What Is and see our current conditions as a possible springboard to what we really want.

Positive change occurs as overcoats fall away and our true, divine nature is able to radiate more brightly.

The outer conditions of our lives automatically mirror our internal shifts.

Change is most likely to happen when we have stopped judging and resisting what is present right now.

As a Sufi aphorism expresses this, *When you can want what you have, you can have what you want.*

Some of the hardest judgments to release are the so-called "spiritual" ones.

"These overcoats should be gone by now."

"I can't believe how caught up in that stuff I still get."

If we heard someone else say these things, we'd hear the judgment, feel the suffering, and provide empathy.

It's time to do that with ourselves.

Whatever is happening in us and our lives IS the process of awakening.

Apparently, it could not happen in any other way, or it would be.

We can let go of any judgments that what is going on is inconvenient, slowing down our awakening, wrong, or bad.

It helps to remember that our "stuff" is not IN the way -- it IS the Way.

When we can meet what is going on with love and acceptance, it becomes part of our path Home.

And that includes all of the judgments weighing us down like the proverbial lead balloon when all we want to do is soar.

Where you are in your spiritual journey must be perfect, or you would be somewhere else.

Picture each of us in a boat floating down the river of awakening.

As we know by now, we are not the ones doing our awakening.

We have no clue how to get that to happen.

It is the love, wisdom and will of the One that propel us around and through the exact obstacles and experiences we need to go through to fully awaken.

Saying, "I want to be on a different river," or "Why is this boat/the scenery/my company the way it is?" only adds to our suffering.

Signing on for the journey, exactly as it is, aligns us with the flow of Life.

That can only make things easier.

As heavy and burdensome as our overcoats often feel, there's no point in judging ourselves for having them.

We came to Earth to experience life here — the good, the bad, and the ugly.

In the process, we accumulated all the overcoats of whatever we were unable to fully experience along the way.

Deep inside, we knew we would eventually learn how to help them fall away and — peekaboo! — reveal our divine nature.

This is just one of a myriad of games souls play within the endless realms of Creation.

Like everything else we are here to experience, it's another adventure in consciousness.

And it feels a lot more like a true adventure and a lot less like an odious task when we do not buy into the judgments that crowd the mind.


## Summing Up

The chapters in this section have presented a simple, straightforward method of being with what is going on within us.

This template of being present with each layer of our inner experience can be used whenever anything even slightly disturbing occurs.

If this process is utilized right away, new layers of overcoats have no reason to accumulate.

We collect the fewest overcoats when we are able to be with what is going on *as it is happening.*

When we can be with what we are experiencing at the time it is taking place, the sensations, feelings, and thoughts move right through us, like waves rippling through the ocean.

Nothing sticks.

Nothing piles up for later.

We are less likely to form judgments about what is going on when we allow our experience to be all of what it is.

We move through life like a small child does, crying when something upsetting happens and laughing a minute later when a parent makes a funny face.

Everything simply is as it is.

No judging, no censoring.

No stopping anything from being just the way it wants to be.

We eat when we're hungry and rest when we're tired.

When tears arise, we let them fall.

When we feel happy, we do not need to know why, or tone it down.

The fountain of energy at our core bubbles up freely and uninhibitedly.

We experience the reasonless happiness and spontaneous joy of the true Self in more and more moments.

This, we discover, is how life was always meant to be.


## Better Late than Never

As helpful as it is to be with What Is at the time it is happening, all is not lost if that was not possible.

Nearly every human being is wearing many overcoats of what could not be fully met when it was unfolding.

The story is never over.

And the overcoats are never too deeply buried to access.

They are waiting for us to bring awareness to them, acknowledge what they contain, and love them into dissolution.

We can always go back to a difficult event or situation later and be with whatever is ready to be felt and released now.

We may revisit an especially troubling issue many times, sloughing off more overcoats each time.

Gradually, the light at our core shines forth more fully as the overcoats of suffering drop away.

# 37

# Turn It ALL Over

*I have always known that I would take this road,*
*but yesterday I did not know that it would be today.*

*Narihira*

In the previous chapters in this section, you have systematically addressed many layers of an issue or challenge.

You gathered the contents of the overcoats related to the situation and turned as much of it over to the Divine as you could.

But there may be more.

As thoroughly as you have looked into the issue, there may be other aspects of the situation that were not addressed through this process.

For instance, many of us carry painful, traumatic memories from past situations and even past lives.

Our minds may contain vivid, disturbing images we have not been able to forget.

Other types of pain and suffering may also be present.

It is possible to gather every bit of this incomplete, unresolved material together and release it all at once.

When we are sincerely ready to be free, there is no reason to hang on to any of this for one more moment.

## Experience: Turn it ALL Over to God

You may have a sense that still more "stuff" surrounding your issue remains to be released.

It doesn't matter if you know what it is or not.

In either case, the process is the same.

Allow your eyes to close and bring your awareness to your breathing.

As you sink into your inner world, invite the situation you are investigating to once again come into your consciousness.

Now, ask all of the facets of it that have not yet been released to come forward.

You may become aware of them, or they may remain diffuse and indistinct.

In either case, feel yourself gathering them all up into a bundle.

Now, give all of it to the Divine.

As you have done before, with the innocence of a little child, let the Divine know that you do not want to hold onto any of it for one more moment.

You might express this in words like these: "God, I don't know what to do with any of this, but I know that I don't want to carry it around any longer. Please take it from me so that I can go free."

Feel yourself releasing it all back into the Whole of Life.

Let it all go.

Breathe it out into the totality of Creation, and see it being reconfigured into pure energy.

Now, notice how you feel within yourself.

Is there a newfound sense of open space where all of this once lived within you?

Are you aware of a fresh sense of possibility, replacing the feeling of doom that once obliterated all hope about the issue?

Enjoy the sensations of freedom that are present.

If any remnants are still there, turn them over as well.

And if more should arise at any point, let them go, too.

## Reflection:

How do you feel now that you have given over whatever remained to be surrendered to the Divine?

Take a few moments to be with yourself and notice any changes in your inner experience.

How does the situation look and feel now?

An issue or challenge is not always neatly resolved in the linear fashion we have employed in the previous chapters.

Bits and pieces of "stuff" may continue to surface for some time after an in-depth exploration feels complete.

At any point, you can face and embrace whatever arises.

Once it has been met with full awareness, you can turn it over to the One.

This is the important thing — that you do not hold on to any of it for a moment longer.

Release it, and feel the Self that you are emerging from beneath even the subtlest layers of overcoats.

## One-Stop Shopping

When things feel complicated and jumbled together, it can be clarifying to separate it all out into the component pieces of the confusing whole.

It can be easier to release the layers of our overcoats when we know what it is we are saying goodbye to.

This is why we focus on distinguishing thoughts and feelings and sensations.

But in the process of getting free, this is not always necessary.

When we are utterly ready to let it all go — when there is nothing we would rather do than leave it all behind — we may not have the patience to separate it all out into its various aspects.

We just want it gone NOW.

The truth is, in **any** situation we face, we can always choose to let it all go, without dissecting it into specific types of content.

Although it is helpful to understand and recognize the various layers of our overcoats, we do not necessarily need to address them one at a time.

As awakening unfolds and we rest in the true Self in more and more moments, we find we would much rather continue to live as That than get busy with overcoats.

So, when overcoats come into our awareness, we may increasingly choose to turn them all over at once.

We are less and less interested in what they are about.

Our fascination with their story is on the wane.

We are ready to walk this Earth free of our overcoats.

We want nothing more than to be clear and transparent, so the light at our core can radiate out into the world and guide all our actions.

When we want to live as who we truly are more than we want to hang on to our overcoats, we can easily and quickly release more than we ever dreamed possible.

# 38

# Forgiveness

*Forgiveness is the fragrance that the violet sheds*
*on the heel that has crushed it.*

*Mark Twain*


Now that you have turned the entire experience over to God, and layer upon layer of overcoats has fallen away, you are more able to look at the situation through the eyes of the eternal soul that you are, instead of through the eyes of your human suffering.

What do you see?

How do the people involved appear to you now?


## Forgiveness of Others

When we see the world through our overcoats, we tend to judge what is going on, believing it should be different.

We also tend to judge the others who are involved.

We may believe they are wrong, bad, or lacking in some way.

We judge and condemn their behavior, or their very beings.

Now that you are looking through the eyes of the Self, is there any truth to that perspective?

Were the people involved in the situation doing the best they could, even if they were acting from their overcoats?

Can any of us be called "bad" and made wrong for what we do not yet understand?

We are all wearing at least a few overcoats of unconsciousness.

Does it make sense to go around judging and condemning one another for that?

Return your awareness to the situation you have been exploring.

What would you say to those people now?

Allow some time for this soulful expression to come forth.

Listening with the ears of the Divine, what would those involved say to you?

Give this all the time it wants.

Seeing everything that took place as you do now, through the eyes of the soul, do you sense the presence of forgiveness within you?

Would you like to express this forgiveness to anyone?

Whether they are still here on Earth or not, you can communicate directly to their hearts and souls.

Let the words arise from your own heart and soul and go out to theirs.

Emotions may also arise and be part of your expression.

Allow the process to continue in its own way.

When it feels complete for now, notice how you feel.

## Self-forgiveness

Now consider how you judged yourself.

Go back over the judgments of yourself you wrote down during the Experience in Chapter Thirty-five.

Notice any feelings of guilt, self-hatred, embarrassment and shame that may remain.

Consider this question:

Were you doing the best you could at the time, considering where you were in your journey of awakening at that point?

How would the Divine view all that happened?

Ask to be shown.

Then ask to see your human self through the eyes of the Self that you are.

What do you see?

Are you ready to release your self-judgments and forgive yourself?

Let that unfold in its own unique way.

How do you feel as the overcoats of judgment fall away?

Go back over the entire incident and see it as you do now, minus the veils of all that once obscured it from your awareness and understanding.

You might like to write about all that you are discovering.


## Forgiving Our Unforgivingness

It is not always easy to forgive.

Years or even decades after a trauma, we may still not be ready and able to forgive.

When deeply damaging events have occurred, we are less likely to quickly and easily let go of our pain and come to forgiveness.

A great deal of inner work may be needed first.

That sacred time with ourselves needs to include plenty of self-empathy and compassion for the pain and suffering we have endured.

This is deep work, requiring time and patience.

While we are immersed in the process of being with ourselves and all of our unresolved feelings, it may make sense to temporarily put forgiveness aside.

The time for that has not yet arrived.

We may have received well-meaning advice to let go and forgive, but we cannot seem to do that yet.

We cannot simply paste a layer of forgiveness over our inner torment.

When feelings continue to arise, they need our love and acceptance, not injunctions to forgive and "get over it."

We will probably need to revisit what happened many times until we can see it through the eyes of the Self, rather than the eyes of the suffering human being.

Only through the eyes of the soul will we see that the others involved were acting out of their own inner torment.

They were damaged, not whole and intact and able to express love.

Only the Self sees that they, too, were suffering, and did not know how to move beyond their own trauma into a peaceful, caring way of being.

Go back to what happened as many times as your awareness takes you there.

Each time, feel the layers of feelings that are now ready to be faced and embraced and felt.

Layer after layer, the overcoats related to this trauma will gradually peel away, allowing more of the divine light that you are to pour into the situation.

Let this process take as long as it needs to take.

Above all, be gentle and patient with yourself.

One day, possibly when you least expect it, you will find yourself experiencing the first taste of authentic forgiveness.

Over time, that forgiveness will continue to deepen until it includes every aspect of what happened, and everyone involved.

This is how we live into the truth Jesus expressed when, in his agony, he implored on behalf of his tormentors, "Forgive them, Father, for they know not what they do."

Forgiveness is as great a gift to ourselves as it is to those we once believed had offended or damaged us.

For when we forgive, we not only stop judging one another.

The overcoats of judgment and condemnation we, ourselves, were wearing fall away, revealing the light that we are.

As more of our divine radiance streams forth, we are less likely to judge the next time it appears someone has wronged us.

And we are less likely to give others a reason to judge our behavior.

They, in turn, are more likely to forgive us.

The self-reinforcing loop of forgiveness literally makes the world a more peaceful, more loving place.

# 39

# When Overcoats Do Not Come Off

*Be patient toward all that is unsolved in your heart*
*and try to love the questions themselves,*
*like locked rooms and like books written in a very foreign tongue...*

Rainer Maria Rilke
*Letters to a Young Poet*

Some overcoats stay stubbornly where they are.

No matter how much we breathe into them and feel what is there, the thoughts and feelings and sensations of suffering stay put.

"Why won't they come off?" we impatiently ask.

But our frustration only piles on more layers of suffering.

Most often, overcoats remain in place because we believe they are who we really are.

Whenever we hear ourselves think or say something like, "This (fill in the blank) is who I am," or "This is the way life is," we have just identified attachment to an overcoat.

This identification is based in one or more beliefs, such as:

*I am my suffering, my history, my trauma, my story.*

*I am a victim, a failure, a hopeless case, a mess.*

*My life is a train wreck. **Again**.*

We unconsciously resist letting go of the overcoat, even though we suffer beneath it, for we fear that without it, we will not be who we are.

Without it, we fear, we may not even exist.

When our suffering continues to recreate itself, we can safely conclude that attachment to our overcoats is the culprit.

We unconsciously fear that if they dissolve away, so will we.

To assess the degree to which this may be the case, try asking yourself:

*Who or what would I be without this image of who I am?*

The answer may surprise you.

## The Glue of Judgment

Our judgments of the overcoats we are wearing also tend to bind them to us.

We may hear inner voices saying things like:

*This shouldn't be going on. I've done so much inner work, it should all be healed by now.*

*What's wrong with me? I thought I'd be over this by now.*

*Other people don't have this issue -- why do I?*

Our judgments of the overcoats do not help the situation.

They merely pile on more layers of overcoats.

And the glue of judgment makes them even harder to let go.

We can stop accumulating more overcoats of judgment by choosing to accept whatever is present within us.

We can decide to love ourselves, right now, just as we are.

We can welcome whatever is wanting to be seen, heard, and known.

Overcoats are not bad or wrong, and we are not bad or wrong for having them.

They simply accumulated when, like most human beings, we didn't know how to fully and lovingly be with their contents when they first appeared.

It is much easier for overcoats to fall away when they are not rejected and made wrong.

Always, the question to ask ourselves is: *Can I love myself, just as I am, with this overcoat?*

An inner voice may respond, "How can I love myself when I'm (fill in the blank)?"

In that question, we can hear the judgment and sense the separation from ourselves.

We can feel the flow of love cutting off to our human experience.

What helps to reopen the flow of love and acceptance is being with each layer of the overcoat.

Step by step, we meet what is there.

We learn that it is possible to simply be with our experience, moment to moment.

This is how we cultivate self-love and compassion for all we've endured.

In that atmosphere of acceptance, all is perfectly fine, just as it is.

# 40

# The No-Fail Spiral of Awakening

*The wisdom of enlightenment is inherent in every
one of us. It is because of the delusion under which
our mind works that we fail to realize it ourselves,
and that we have to seek the advice and the
guidance of enlightened ones.*

*Hui Neng*

We nurture our ability to empathize with ourselves when we remember that awakening does not unfold in an ever-upward straight line.

It is a cyclical, spiraling process that loops back around to places we have visited before, again and again.

And again.

It can seem as through we are making no progress.

We judge ourselves and wonder why we are back at the same place, feeling the same feelings we've felt so many times before.

*I thought I was done with this!*

*I'm tired of feeling these feelings!*

*Is there something wrong with me?*

*I can't seem to get through this.*

Our minds often hold an impossible ideal:

*I should have been able to get through it all the first time I dealt with it.*

But the truth is, no one could possibly face and embrace *everything* about a traumatic incident or life passage all at once.

That is a seriously unrealistic expectation.

There are inevitably layers of overcoats and aspects of what went on that we just aren't ready to face -- until we are.

It's a lot like unraveling a ball of tangled-up yarn.

We can't undo the knots near the center until we deal with the ones on the surface.

We work our way toward the most challenging aspects of what happened, and they reveal themselves as we are ready to face them.

That process can take years, and sometimes decades.

We may even have explored some evolutionary challenges for lifetimes.

So we can let go of all evaluations and judgments on ourselves, and realize the process will unfold in God's time, according to God's assessment of what we're ready to face now...and now...and now.

When we think we know more than the Divine about how things should be going, we are setting ourselves up for more suffering.

And piling on more overcoats!

So, if we seem to be traveling over the same ground we've visited many times before, we can remind ourselves that we are not failing, and this is not a disaster.

It is to be expected.

More overcoats of suffering are about to fall away.

And new levels of awareness are about to dawn on us.

At every turn of the spiral, we can remember this:

If something is present -- a closed-down part of the body, a thought, a feeling, a judgment -- it doesn't matter how many times we've looked at it or felt it before; it is not yet complete.

When it has received all that it needs from us, it moves through and releases.

If it is still there, it needs something more from us.

Most often, what that suffering part of us is waiting for is love -- not just a crumb of acceptance tossed its way, or a token five minutes spent breathing and feeling.

The wounded, suffering parts of us yearn to be bathed in the deep love and compassion we all hope to receive for what we have endured in this life.

What we crave is not a carefully meted-out thimble-full of love.

We all know everything we need to know about what that feels like.

What we yearn to receive is an everblooming extravagance of love, a full-on cascading waterfall of it, tumbling over us.

Each of us deserves nothing less than an oceanic tidal wave of utterly-without-limits love.

Awash in that tsunami of love, no overcoat stands a chance of continuing to hide the light that we are.

This deluge of love happens automatically as we fall more deeply into the soul's home in our heart of hearts.

As we come to know beyond all doubt that **we are** the Self.

The Divine Love at our core enfolds our human self and all that we have been through with the tenderest, gentlest embrace imaginable.

As we lavish ourselves with love the way a five-year-old would frost a cake, we develop the essential spiritual muscles of radical, extreme loving-kindness and compassion.

What more important muscles could we ever want?

Now, we come to know the indomitable strength of the true Self.

We realize we **are** the power that can love whatever arises.

When we see our human selves through the compassionate eyes of the Self, we realize we are doing the best we can with this life of ours.

With each turn of the spiral, we have reached a new level of awareness.

We see more clearly what went on during the painful moments.

We feel a little more of what couldn't be felt before, and we more fully let the feelings go each time.

We release more of our clinging and attachment to whatever happened as something that defines who we are.

With each return to the event, we slough off more layers of overcoats -- body-sensations, beliefs, emotions, judgments, and all the rest.

Each time we spiral back to that moment in time, we have an opportunity to celebrate how far we've come.

That feels a whole lot more satisfying than using it as yet another excuse to beat ourselves up for not being "further along."

# 41

# Neti, Neti

*Since everything is but an apparition,*
*perfect in being what it is,*
*having nothing to do with good or bad,*
*acceptance or rejection,*
*one may well burst out in laughter.*

*Longchenpa*

Awakening has been described in a multitude of ways.

For centuries, spiritual seekers and teachers have discussed and debated how awakening happens and what helps it along.

For the purposes of this book, we'll stick to Gurudeva's simple description.

To paraphrase the beloved Hindu master, awakening means realizing that *we are not our overcoats -- we are the light, love and life of God, shining out from within our individualized forms.*

Simply put, awakening equals realizing that we are more than the being we see in the mirror.

**We are not what that being looks like.**

**And we are not what that being has experienced.**

*We are not our suffering.*

*We are not our accomplishments.*

*We are not our failures.*

*We are not our neuroses or psychoses.*

*We are not our diseases -- or our health.*

*We are not the roles we play.*

*We are not our thoughts.*

*We are not our feelings.*

*We are not the sensations we experience all throughout the day.*

*We are not our friends, or our families, or our jobs, or our homes.*

## Not This, Not That

If we are none of this, then who are we?

What remains when we strip all of this away?

When we believe we are our physical appearance, or our home, or our closest relationship, if that element of our life changes or goes away, we feel diminished in *who we are*.

We have not only lost a valued aspect of our lives -- we believe we have lost *a part of ourselves*.

When we identify with the light at our core as who we are, all other facets of our life experience can come and go and we will still rest in our true nature.

While everything else may change, the light at our center never comes and goes.

No matter what happens, we are always who we are.

Nothing can take that away.

In India, there is a saying for the transitory aspects of life: *neti, neti.*

It translates as, "Not this, not that."

*Neti, neti* reminds us that **I am not my body.**

**I am not my feelings.**

**I am not my mind.**

**I am not any aspect of my being or experience that is impermanent.**

Gurudeva's story reminds us that we are not our overcoats -- we are the eternal, divine light beneath them.

We are the unchanging essence, not the ever-changing surface appearance.


## Overcoats R Not Us!

Who are we without our overcoats?

What remains when we shed those layers of not-self?

The next section of the book is about coming home to who we really are.

Remember, there is nothing we need to do, seek, or find.

Nothing to add, change, or fix.

In a well-known fable, a man stands admiring a sculptor's magnificent statue of an elephant.

The man asks, "How did you do it?"

The sculptor famously replies, "That's simple -- I merely chipped away everything that is not the elephant."

That is exactly what we are doing as we remove our overcoats.

We are shedding everything that is not who we truly are.

As we continue to bring awareness to all that we are not, more and more of who we really are stands forth, freed from the veiling that has obscured our divine magnificence.

We see it, and the world sees it.

And just as there are ways to expedite overcoat removal -- ways with which you are becoming intimately familiar -- there are also ways to enhance your experience of your true nature.

The next section of the book is all about these technologies of consciousness.

They will allow you to more fully experience the divine magnificence of who you truly are.

We are far more than the absence of overcoats!

# PART SIX

❖ ❖ ❖

# The Divine Self Revealed: Experiencing Who We Really Are

❖ ❖ ❖

# 42

# The True Self

*Finally I am coming to the conclusion*
*that my highest ambition is to be what I already am.*

*Thomas Merton*

So often in this human life, all we are aware of is our over-coats.

Looking in the mirror, the light at our core is not what we see.

Instead, we perceive only our flaws -- everything we have not yet accepted about our outer appearance.

Or we see our mask self, the carefully contrived edifice we hope will impress the world.

When we bring awareness to our inner world, our inner light is not usually what we see or sense first.

Traveling inward, we encounter the tangled web of our suffering.

Issue upon issue, challenge after challenge, have piled up countless overcoats.

And it is all too easy to forget that none of them has any-thing to do with who we really are.

In the state of being that most humans experience, overcoats are just about all we ever know.

It is easy to conclude that our overcoats are the only reality that exists.

## Realizing the True Self

The overcoats of our human dilemma may have become so thick and solid, we can barely believe that the brilliant light of the true Self is even there within us.

Yet there isn't a human being among us who hasn't, however fleetingly, experienced the divine essence that lives in us all.

Many of us glimpsed the truth of our nature as children, before the world impinged upon that incandescent reality.

You may have felt the light of your innermost core beaming out in joy when you played make-believe, or observed the mystery of tadpoles morphing into frogs, or romped with a beloved pet.

Later in life, you might have felt an ineffable something coming alive inside as you gazed out over a stunningly beautiful vista.

The rays of the setting sun refracting through the clouds ignited your own inner radiance, and you tasted ecstasy, if only for a brief moment in time.

Or you felt your oneness with God while flying down a mountain or standing in a stream or digging in the dirt or doing whatever it is that you love to do.

The following Experience is designed to evoke the moments in your life when you knew beyond all doubt that the Divine lives in you as your true, eternal Self.

When you lived and loved as That.

## Experience: Remembering the True Self

Invite your body to come into a comfortable position, and place your notebook or journal nearby.

Read these directions now and refer to them during the process as needed.

As your eyes gently close, become aware of your breathing.

Let your breath and your awareness carry you into your inner world.

Now, ask to be made aware of a time when you were very much aware of your divine core.

You were experiencing life as your true Self.

It was as if the radiance of your innermost core blasted through all of your overcoats and made them irrelevant, if only for a short time.

This may have occurred when you met your life partner, or were present at the birth of your child.

It might have happened when you first experienced a place on the planet that felt like Home.

Or when you participated in an activity that felt like a perfect soul-expression for you.

Whatever it was, allow yourself to become aware of it now.

If more than one experience is arising, choose one to begin with and go back to the others later.

See yourself there, and feel what it was like.

Be present in that time as though it is right now.

Notice the inner subtle feelings of aliveness.

What do you see?

Are touch or taste involved?

Smell any aromas that are part of the experience.

Let it come fully alive for you.

What are you experiencing?

Which aspects of your innermost essence are stimulated by what is going on?

You might be in touch with the love, the light, the joy, the bliss, the deep peace, or some other facet of who you really are.

Allow yourself to savor every bit of this experience.

When you feel complete with this moment in time, ask for another to be brought into your awareness.

Fully experience it as if it were happening now.

Let yourself feel the way you, as your true Self, experienced this event.

Continue revisiting times when you were very aware of *being* your true Self until you feel complete for now.

You might like to journal about what made these moments the profound experiences they were.


## Reflection:

What does it feel like when you are experiencing life as your true Self?

What are the qualities that make those moments so precious to you?

Now imagine a life in which these moments weave together to create a solid fabric.

Imagine what it will be like to consistently and ever more completely live as your true Self.

# 43

# Moving Toward the True Self

*There is a light that shines beyond all things on earth,*
*beyond us all, beyond the heavens,*
*beyond the highest, the very highest heavens.*
*This is the Light that shines in our heart.*

Chandogya Upanishad

The Self is not a place in consciousness we occasionally visit.

It is not someplace we hope to get to someday.

It is not *out there* somewhere in a mysterious realm.

In truth, **we are** the true Self.

Something in us may not want to believe such an affirming view of ourselves.

Yet working over time with the Experience in the previous chapter has the power to replace all former identities with the truth of who we really are.

When we have identified with our overcoats -- and who among us hasn't? -- it takes a radical shift in consciousness to realize we are light, we are love, we are life.

Jesus said, "I AM the Light of the world."

And so are we.

Centuries ago, people were imprisoned, tortured, and burned at the stake for declaring themselves to be one with God.

This was considered outrageous blasphemy.

The fear of what would happen if we spoke the truth silenced more than a few of us in other lifetimes.

And when we came out with what we knew to be true, millions of us were killed.

Traces of these experiences may linger in our psyches, preventing us from standing confidently in the magnificent reality of our true nature.

We may face deep-seated fears of what might happen if we abandon our disguises.

It might seem safer to remain enshrouded within and identified with our overcoats.

However, living from our overcoats means we continue to suffer and perpetuate suffering.

In contrast, living from the true Self lets us find out what it is like to thrive and blossom.

How do we shift from identifying with our overcoats to *knowing,* all the way up and all the way down, that **we are** the true Self?

Although becoming skilled at helping overcoats to peel away is vital, it's not everything.

Reading about awakening is only part of the story.

We also need to have our own experiences of awakening.

This is the only way we will really *get* who we are.

Ultimately, the goal of the spiritual journey is merging fully with and knowing that we **are** the luminous presence of our true Self in the core of our being.

Taking off overcoats is a pathway to this, the ultimate point of it all.

To live as the incandescent, inextinguishable light that we are makes everything we have experienced along the way worth it.

So how do we segue from an intellectual understanding that we *are* the true Self to a deep, unshakable *knowing* of that as the ground of our being?

Consider your immersion into the Self during the previous chapter's Experience.

Feeling the presence of the Divine within yourself begins to shift your sense of self from identifying with your overcoats to knowing yourself as essence, soul, Self.

Many people say they feel their true Self outside of their physical form -- surrounding them in their aura or energy field, or somewhere above themselves.

And it is true that the Self is too vast to be confined to a specific location.

However, for the purposes of this book, we'll focus on experiencing the true Self *within* the physical form.

Directly experiencing that the Self lives within the physical body has a profound effect on people.

For if we can breathe and feel the presence of our overcoats, we can also breathe and feel the presence of the Self.

# 44

# Experiencing the True Self

*Deep within you is everything that is perfect,*
*ready to radiate through you*
*and out into the world.*

*A Course in Miracles, Lesson 41*

## The Soul Lotus, the Abode of the True, Eternal Self

At the sacred center of each one of us lies the Soul Lotus, the primary focal-point of the drop of the Divine that you are.

This is where most people experience the presence of the Self within their physical form.

For as long as the Self wishes to experience life in a physical body, it keeps our heart beating and our lungs breathing.

The Self maintains all other bodily functions as well as it can until the moment arrives for us to leave the body and return Home.

Within the Soul Lotus, the true, eternal Self is constantly orchestrating all that goes on at every level of our existence.

This innermost sacred space is the Holy of Holies of our being.

Everything that God is lives within the divine flame in the Soul Lotus.

All the intelligence, wisdom, and power of Source can be accessed within this sacred center.

Everything that each one of us has been seeking -- love, joy, wisdom, happiness, peace -- is already here within us.

These qualities are our true nature.

The Soul Lotus is the temple of the radiant, divine Self that lives beneath all of our overcoats, as Gurudeva assured his long-ago audience.

One aspect of awakening is releasing the overcoats that hide the Self.

The other aspect of awakening is merging our consciousness with and knowing we **are** the true, eternal Self.

## Where is the Soul Lotus?

The Soul Lotus lies an inch or two above the physical heart, in the center of the chest.

People in many cultures bring the palms of their hands together over this sacred space when they pray.

When we are moved by something, one of our hands may spontaneously rise to cover this place in our upper chest.

Placing a hand over this area is a simple, powerful way to help our awareness focus here.

## How Does the Soul Lotus Open?

Until we are ready to realize the Self as our true identity, the Soul Lotus is held nearly closed beneath the heavy overcoats we believe are who we are.

As we begin to awaken and overcoats drop away, the dense veiling around the Soul Lotus dissipates, enabling it to open and expand.

This allows us to more fully experience the presence of God in our sacred core.

We become ever more aware that divinity lives within us as our true nature.

The Soul Lotus blossoms as we increasingly experience the presence of the true Self and identify with it, not the human self, as who we really are.

As the Soul Lotus opens, the presence of God pours forth, infusing our entire being with all aspects of our true nature.

The divine qualities of the Self — love, peace, joy, equanimity, clarity, and many more — permeate our earthly experience in more and more moments.

The exalted characteristics and unlimited capacities of the One begin to manifest through our human expression.

In beings like Jesus, Buddha, Krishna, and other fully awakened souls, the Soul Lotus is fully blooming, radiating divinity through each and every action and expression.

## Experiencing the True Self in the Soul Lotus

Like everything that occurs as we awaken, experiencing the Self in the Soul Lotus happens through Grace.

The Divine calls us Home and leads us there, step by step.

It knows the perfect path for each one of us.

Surrendering to the Grace of the Divine and inviting That to lead you to your innermost center is the Way.

The journey will take you through one overcoat after another, revealing more and more of your true, eternal Self.

Moving toward our inner sanctum is something like entering into the hushed interior of a cathedral or temple.

Outside the temple, we first must pass by statues of the fearsome gargoyles or wrathful deities guarding the entrance.

They represent the daunting fears and paralyzing judgments we may encounter in ourselves as we venture inward toward the abode of the Self.

Once we make it past these apparitions, we may have to walk down a long corridor before the door opens to the innermost sacred center of the structure.

The hallways is long enough to cause us to question whether we really want to continue on.

Is it that important to us?

Most humans do not enter the inner sanctum of the Soul Lotus until enough overcoats have fallen away that we begin to glimpse our inner light.

Finally, in one lifetime or another, the time comes when entering into the Holy of Holies within ourselves is our next evolutionary step.

We may still feel some angst and trepidation, but our desire to directly experience who we really are is strong enough to overcome these obstacles.


## Is it time?

All of the consciousness skills you have been cultivating will assist you to move through the layers of overcoats toward the Soul Lotus.

You are more able now to greet whatever presents itself in a friendly, welcoming way, rather than viewing it as wrong or bad.

You know that what is present is not IN the way -- it IS the Way.

You also know that nothing in any of the overcoats is ultimately real or true, and none of it has any power over you.

If an overcoat arises, you trust that facing it must be part of your path Home.

So you meet it with love and invite it to reveal itself to you.

As you get to know the overcoat and all it contains, you no longer fear becoming trapped within its layers.

Instead, you remember to *breathe, feel, witness, and turn it over to God.*

As overcoats unravel and dissolve, you are propelled toward the inner sanctum of the Soul Lotus.

Deep within that sacred space burns the eternal flame of the divine Self.

Is it time to begin the journey into your innermost Home?

## Experience: Moving Toward the Home of the Self, the Soul Lotus

PART ONE: Preparing for the Journey

Let your body find a comfortable position, preferably sitting upright, and place your journal nearby.

Read these directions and refer back to them as needed throughout the process.

Allow your awareness to rest on your breath, feeling each breath coming in and going out through your nostrils.

As your eyes gently close, feel your consciousness turning inward.

Invite a few breaths to come and go while your awareness settles into your inner landscape.

If emotions, thoughts, or bodily sensations arise, with each in-breath, breathe into them and feel whatever is present.

On each out-breath, turn the sensations over to the Divine.

Allow this process to continue until sensations fall away and a space of relative quiet is reached.

Become aware of your entire body now, as you continue to breathe and feel whatever is present.

Feel your intention to travel deeper within, to the Holy of Holies at your core -- the Soul Lotus, where the true, eternal Self focalizes within your physical form.

Feel how much you would like to experience your inner-most divine nature.

Then, realize two things.

One: You do not know how to make this happen.

And Two: That is OK.

The truth is, there is no way any of us can "do" this on our own.

We all need divine grace to show us the Way.

The time has come to turn the entire experience over to the One Who Knows how to facilitate it best.

Ask the Divine to lead you toward the Soul Lotus, the abode of the Self, in the way that is perfect for you right now.

And give thanks for the assistance you are about to receive.

PART TWO: Moving Toward the True Self in the Soul Lotus

Begin by inviting your breath into the area of your chest that is above and behind your physical heart.

This is where the Soul Lotus is already beginning to blossom within you.

You might like to place a hand over this part of your body.

This will help your awareness to stay focused there.

As a few breaths come and go, feel the sensations that are present in this part of your being.

With each in-breath, feel what is there.

On each out-breath, let the sensations go.

Turn them over to God.

Let each breath soften and open the area in your upper chest.

Again, feel how much you want to experience the divine core of your being.

Know that whatever arises is part of the path Home.

Nothing is extraneous; nothing needs to be rejected.

Whether feelings or thoughts or distracting sensations arise, know that they are all part of the process or they wouldn't be there.

These are all layers of the overcoats that are ready to fall away today.

Surrender into the mysterious unfoldment of the journey.

Let go of the steering wheel.

You are not doing this -- the Divine is.

Now, invite the Soul Lotus to come forth into your aware-ness.

See it, feel it, sense it, in whatever ways it presents itself to you.

Enjoy beholding this flower of holiness deep within your being.

This is the sacred abode, the innermost home, of the Self that you are.

Ask the Soul Lotus to open and reveal the Divine within.

Invite the true, eternal Self to come forth in whatever ways it likes.

All you need to do is maintain your awareness in the area of the Soul Lotus and be receptive to whatever ways the soul begins to come forth.

It may present itself through a feeling, a light, a symbol, or in some other manner.

A deep peace and stillness may come over you.

You may have an indescribable sensation of the unique essence of your being -- that which makes you **you**.

You might sense the Soul Lotus opening, like a flower, revealing the light of the true Self at its core.

Allow some time now to be present with whatever unfolds.

Let yourself fully enjoy the merging of your human self with your true, eternal Self.

Invite the breath to amplify the sensations and experiences taking place within the Soul Lotus.

Let whatever is happening expand and continue for as long as it likes.

Let yourself *have* and *savor* everything that is a part of your experience.

If it seems as though nothing is happening, just continue to breathe and feel whatever is present.

If overcoats of thought and feeling arise, witness them, feel them, and turn them over to God.

Remember, believing the thoughts and judgments is optional.

You may encounter some overcoats, and then glimpse or feel your divine essence.

Then, more overcoat layers may surface.

Self-judgments may arise:

*I'm not doing this right.*

*Other people are able to do this, but not me.*

Then, another waft of essence.

Peace.

Stillness.

The journey usually alternates between these two primary facets of the process.

Rarely does it progress in a straight line, or land permanently in the home of the soul.

Instead, your awareness will probably meander through your inner landscape in a wandering, nonlinear fashion.

When you are open to the mystery, unpredictable blessings often arrive.

Continue to turn the entire process over to the Divine.

Trust that it is unfolding in the right way for you at this time.

Breathe, feel, and drop more deeply into being present within your divine core.

Just for a moment -- or maybe forever -- feel the sacred essence of **you** that shines forth when all overcoats fall away.

Feel the expansiveness of your true nature.

You are experiencing yourself as the Self.

This is what is most real and true about you.

When we rest in the Self, we **know** this is who we really are.

Remind yourself, "If I hang on to these overcoats, who I really am remains hidden."

Enjoy coming out of hiding!

Let your awareness rest in the sacred space above your heart for as long as you like.

Glory in the unique essence of the Divine that is your true Self.

Affirm that you **are** this!

Rest in your true nature for as long as you like.

## Reflection:

Your initial experiences of the Soul Lotus and the true Self are likely to be subtle.

Our outer-directed awareness is used to big, dramatic events and phenomena, and may expect more of the same from the inner landscape.

But such expectations often lead to disappointment and self-judgment.

Far better to drop all ideas about how the Self will come forth and let that unfold in its own way.

As we attune to the inner world over time, we are increasingly able to perceive the subtleties of the soul realms.

The Self may come forth as the *absence* of the noise and confusion of human life.

Especially when we need a respite from the cacophony of earthly existence, dropping into the Self can feel like entering into the Void.

If we have become puffed up with the fullness of human life, we may need to experience the divine Self as a zero — nothing and nobody.

This kind of experience might lead you to believe that not much is happening, when, in fact, you have tasted the exquisite subtlety of the Self.

"Nothing happening" often turns out to be a glimpse, or a longer immersion, into the endless peace and deep stillness of the soul.

How often do any of us experience that in our outer lives?

Most of us yearn for that peace, yet when it is actually present we may decide that nothing is happening.

Thinking something else should be going on, we may conclude we are deficient, "not spiritual enough" to experience the soul realms.

We might even judge the experience — and our awakening — as a fail.

How quickly the mind jumps in with its judgments!

In its compassionate wisdom, the Self presents itself to us exactly as we most need to experience it.

As the Soul Lotus blossoms, the unique frequencies of our true nature pour forth from our sacred center to infuse our entire being with the energy~consciousness of the Self.

We may be filled with its love, or bask in its light.

Wisdom and knowing may flood into our consciousness, providing the answers to questions we weren't even sure how to ask.

Our experiences of the Self reflect what our human self is ready to open to at each moment in our journey of awakening.

Sometimes these experiences are clearly gifts of grace that we welcome with gratitude and even wonder.

At other times, the Self may seem paradoxical and puzzling, for it expresses levels of awareness beyond those with which we are familiar.

In any case, the more we open to the Self, the more our consciousness is expanded and enlarged.

And the more we remember the vastness and magnificence of who and what we truly are.

## The Shift from Overcoats to Self

Because we have been so identified with our overcoats, most of us are not firmly established in the true Self after one immersion within the Soul Lotus.

Through repeated experiences of the divinity at our core, we progressively realize that *this* is who we truly are, not our overcoats.

We will travel back and forth, over and over, between our overcoats and our essential Self.

Each time we venture into overcoat-land, we see a little more clearly how they got there and what we need to know and experience so they can fall away.

And every time we return to the refuge of the Soul Lotus, the sacred center of our true being, the focus of our awareness becomes more deeply established in the Self that we are.

The radiance of our true nature progressively burns away our overcoats.

We literally out-radiate them.

Over time, we journey into overcoat-land less and less, as we live more and more fully from our innermost essence.

Overcoats of thought, feeling, and judgment will continue to arise, but we know they are not who we are.

And we are blessed to live in more and more moments as the radiant Self that is our true identity.


## The Blossoming of the Self

Even if it seemed that not much happened during your journey into the Soul Lotus, do not despair.

Sometimes our expectations get in the way of noticing and appreciating what actually did take place.

Some people imagine the realms of the Self will be suffused with ethereal magic, complete with angelic choirs and heavenly special effects.

In reality, the domain of the soul rests in stillness and peace.

It has nothing to do with the spiritual glamour we may be expecting.

When we grasp this truth and accept it, we may actually feel relieved.

Letting go of our concepts and expectations, we can invite the soul to reveal itself in its own beautifully subtle way.

And we can trust that when this is what we want more than anything, it will happen.

In a garden, every flower blooms in its own timing and way.

It doesn't matter where we are in the blossoming process.

Whether the bud of our Soul Lotus is barely opening, half-open, or exuberantly open wide, the truth is that we, and our awakening, are blossoming.


## Resting in the Self

Resting in who we really are is the core of awakening.

In the process, the human self merges with and dissolves into the true Self.

Yogis and mystics devote their lives to this.

They may rest in the Self for hours a day, until all aspects of their being are unified within the true Self.

Basking in the radiance and love of the soul can become the core of your daily meditation time.

This supports awakening to who you really are more than any other practice.

All along the way, overcoats will fall away and the light of the Self will shine forth more fully.

Over time, you will be blessed with more and more moments of simply resting in the Divine Self that you are, focalized within the Soul Lotus.

What could be better than that?

In this timeless sacred space, there is nothing to do and no one to do it.

All simply arises and then falls away, observed from within your Holy of Holies.

Thoughts come and go, but it is clear they have nothing to do with who you truly are.

When feelings arise, it is no problem to let them move through and release.

Nothing that is external to your essence sticks or has any lasting reality.

In this space, the impermanent nature of all passing phenomena is clearly revealed.

This imparts the deep truth that the only ultimate reality is that of the true Self.

As you awaken, you realize that giving energy to your overcoats makes as much sense as believing the movie you saw last night was real.


## Living Life as the Soul

Resting in the Self progressively unfolds over time.

At first, our awareness is frequently pulled out into our overcoats.

We identify with what is in them, believing we are our pain and suffering.

Only rarely do we glimpse the Self that we really are.

As awakening blossoms, we increasingly find ourselves peacefully resting in the Self.

Becoming caught up in our overcoats happens less and less.

Each time you bring awareness to the space in the upper chest where the Soul Lotus is located, even if you are not aware of much happening, stay with your intention and deep desire to experience the sacred core of your being.

Reaffirm your yearning to live as who you really are in this world that is so largely run by overcoats.

This world that is so in need of what lies beneath them all.

Living as a soul, not as your overcoats, may be the most important contribution you can make to the Whole.

And on the days when the light of the soul seems to be hopelessly buried beneath the overcoats, be gentle with yourself.

Turn all of your feelings of impatience, frustration and hopelessness over to the Divine.

And give your life over to your true Self.

Ask your divine essence to come forth in whatever ways it likes, in the timing that is right for that.

You may have definite, radiant inner experiences of the Self, or the Self may come forth in other, less immediately obvious ways.

You might find yourself feeling more at peace about your issues and challenges.

Daily life may take on a new quality of calmness, or joy, or harmony.

Your buttons may not be pushed as often, and when you are triggered, you react less.

You may become more self-accepting, and more able to love others as they are.

Moments of reasonless happiness and gratitude are likely to occur more often.

Setting aside time each day to rest in the Self reminds us as nothing else can that we are not the body we see in the mirror.

We are the radiance at its sacred center.

Remembering this, *living* as this, will make it far easier to let the body go when the time comes for that.

Meanwhile, be on the lookout for signs that the soul is taking dominion over your life.

Notice the waning power your overcoats have to control your awareness and convince you their agendas are real.

Feel the radiance at your core shining out in more and more moments.

See yourself living as the ever more fully embodied Self that you are.

Knowing that you are the Self has the power to alter your experience like nothing else possibly can.

## Our Soul Purpose and Destiny

As souls, each of us came to Earth not only to slough off overcoats and remember who we are, but also to bring something to the planet no one else can offer in quite the same way.

The great joy of awakening is to feel this gift rising up inside, and to bring it forth to bless the world.

As one of us fulfills our soul destiny and purpose, the path into full soul-expression is widened for us all.

Imagine what the world will be like when all of us are expressing the unique gifts we are here to add to the Whole.

What we do today — what we **are** today — is helping to bring that world forth.

By embracing the contents of our overcoats and then letting them go, we are helping to birth a more soulful, loving world.

Every time we slough off another overcoat, it becomes easier for everyone else to release theirs.

Although the details differ, we are all wearing the same kinds of overcoats.

That's because there is really only One of us here.

And as each layer of each overcoat falls away, the brilliant light at our core shines out into the world a little more brightly.

Each time we remind ourselves that our overcoats are not who we are, we awaken a little more fully.

Our ever-brighter radiance sparks the light in those we meet who are ready for that to happen.

As we grow brighter, those around us grow brighter.

## The End...and the Beginning

Eventually, we will all outshine every one of our earthly trials and challenges.

We will have fulfilled all of our purposes for taking incarnation.

More and more of our overcoats will have fallen away, until the light at our core shines out like a lighthouse for all to see.

Our reasons for coming to Earth, lifetime after lifetime, will have vanished.

Our game of make-believe will be over.

Now it is time to return Home.

The physical body is the last overcoat each of us will shed. As we let the body go, what will remain is the light that we are.

Leaving this Earth, our light will be reabsorbed into the Great Light of the One.

We will exist as light and nothing but light.

Light...love...consciousness...oneness.

No more pain, no more suffering.

How beautiful it will be to float endlessly in our true nature!

That makes all that we went through along the way completely worth it.

For every bit of it brought us into this eternal moment.

And we couldn't have arrived here without the journey out from our Source and back again.

The journey of piling on overcoats, and learning how to let them go.

The journey of forgetting who we are, and remembering again.

The journey of hiding our light, and then, at last, letting it shine.

# Afterword

# Going Deeper in Taking Off Overcoats

Now that you've reached the end of the book, your journey of awakening is by no means over. We highly recommend that you continue to work with the practices presented here on a regular basis. The many Experiences in Parts Four, Five, and Six of the book are especially supportive of awakening. As you become more and more familiar with them, you'll likely find that some will become cornerstones of your daily sacred time. In the process, they will become a part of you, as natural and unthinking as breathing.

Remember, in each moment you are either experiencing the truth of your being — the radiant peace and vibrant stillness of the True Self — or you are in the experience of one or more overcoats, the layers of who you are not. As you deepen in the Self over time, you will become better able to spot and dis-identify with the overcoats you thought were who you are.

But sometimes overcoats look and feel so real and convincing, it may seem impossible to extricate yourself from them on your own. Expert facilitation can make all the difference between succumbing to hopelessness and despair, and breaking through to the freedom of awakening. Whenever you reach such an impasse, we encourage you to contact us for a private session.

For decades, we have walked alongside people as they shed the overcoats of suffering and rediscover the solace of the soul. We have traveled into the very deepest realms of pain and suffering — not once in a while, but so often we have learned one vital truth: **There is nothing that cannot be faced, embraced, and moved through, if we are willing to meet it with full Presence and turn it over to the Divine for help.** We have never found **anything** that did not shift and open through the alchemical power of divine love.

People tell us the energy~consciousness space we hold and the quality of our presence are vital ingredients in the major shifts and openings they experience during sessions. Those who do ongoing work with us naturally begin to entrain to this quality of presence and embody it themselves over time. This is a direct result of invoking Help from Beyond, for the more fully we immerse in the Divine, the more It expresses in us and our lives.

If diving more deeply into your suffering with us feels scary, please imagine trying to continue living with it gnawing at you inside. What is the point in that? We are not meant to suffer our way through this life. You might find **this video** on our Home Page (https://www.luminousself.com/) to be helpful. In it, we discuss the many reasons people hesitate to contact us for sessions, none of which has any ultimate truth or reality.

Fear can stop us from risking the unknown and taking chances that turn out to be liberating. Fear can close us off to possibilities that open the doors into the life we know is possible and yearn to experience. As you now know from reading this book, fear is just another inner experience, and can be faced, embraced, and gone beyond. We do not need to let our fear of our fear stop us!

Often, fear is the first doorway people encounter in sessions. Instead of trying to banish fear or making it wrong, we explore it together in a safe, sacred space of healing. In countless sessions, we have never met a fear that did not give way to greater life, love, and freedom. Very often, facing our fears also invites our inner wisdom to come forth, showing us the Way through it to greater self-love and freedom from suffering.

If we could say one thing to you, it would be this: **Don't let your fear stop you from pursuing something that offers you everything you know is possible but aren't sure how to find on your own.** One or more sessions with us can mean the difference between continuing to suffer in stuckness and unhappiness, and accessing your inner wellspring of life, light, and joy.

You are meant to blossom and thrive. From our hearts, we invite you to **contact us** for a free, 20-minute consultation or to set up a session.

# Endnotes

## Chapter One: The Story

Gurudeva's full spiritual name is Satguru Sivaya Subramuniyaswami. He lived from 1927–2001. For more about Gurudeva and his lineage, along with a wonderful photograph of this beloved teacher, go to **http://www.himalayanacademy.com/monastery/lineage-philosophy/gurudeva**.

## Chapter Fifteen: The Veils that Obscure the True Self

**"The Burden of our Overcoats" section:** We believe John Welwood was the first to write about the phenomenon of spiritual bypassing. More recently, Robert Augustus Masters wrote *Spiritual Bypassing: When Spirituality Disconnects Us from What Really Matters* (2010, North Atlantic books).

## Chapter Twenty: Judgments

**"Fake Feeling-statements" section:** The books and teachings of the late Marshall Rosenberg provide excellent guidance on the clear and accurate expression of feelings. See especially *Nonviolent Communication: A Language of Life*, Puddle Dancer Press, 2003. The extensive lists of feelings on pages 44 and 45 of this classic are invaluable in learning the language of feelings and avoiding fake feeling statements, otherwise known as judgments.

For much more on finding the way to freedom from judgment, explore the Work and the books of Byron Katie. *Loving What Is*, her first book, is a good place to start.

# Acknowledgements

A bow of thanks to Anna Oneglia for her vibrant, colorful cover illustration.

Many thanks to DeeDee Schneider, who read an early draft of this book and provided valuable feedback and suggestions.

A warm mahalo to Alana Wolfe, who provided detailed comments that greatly improved our previous books and strengthened our ability to write clearly.

Our deep gratitude to all the awakening souls we have been blessed to walk alongside during individual sessions, groups, and teleconferences.

This book would not exist without the Divine Source from which it flowed so easily and effortlessly. Endless thanks to the One from which all within Creation emanates!

81610765R00204

Made in the USA
San Bernardino, CA
09 July 2018